James Study Guide

James
STUDY GUIDE

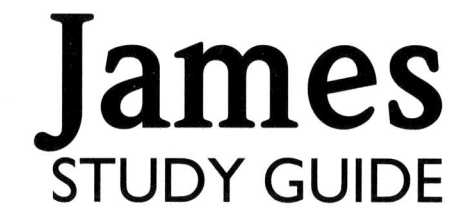

Michael Lewis

The Christadelphian
404 Shaftmoor Lane, Hall Green, Birmingham B28 8SZ, UK
© 2013 The Christadelphian Magazine and Publishing Association.

First published 2013
ISBN 978 0 85189 231 3 (Print edition)
ISBN 978 0 85189 232 0 (Electronic edition)

Printed and bound in Malta by:
Gutenberg Press Ltd.

Contents

What is a Study Guide?	vi	**7 The role of the teacher**	27
Preface	vii	Chapter 3	
1 Introduction	1	**8 Strife – the cause and cure**	33
2 Justification by faith	5	Chapter 4	
3 Overview	9	**9 Patience and prayer**	39
4 The foundations of faith	13	Chapter 5	
Chapter 1		**10 Do good to all**	45
5 The royal law	19	**11 Outline answers to questions**	53
Chapter 2 verses 1 to 13		**Further reading**	54
6 The living faith	23		
Chapter 2 verses 14 to 26			

What is a Study Guide?

1. **Aims:** The overriding aim of all Bible study is that through knowledge and understanding of the word of God a person may become *"wise for salvation through faith which is in Christ Jesus"* (2 Timothy 3:15).

   "Study Guides" are designed to explain the straightforward teachings of scripture and where appropriate to emphasise:

   a) First principles of doctrine

   b) Practical outcomes

   They should be helpful to young people, to those who are new to the faith, who often have little background knowledge of the Bible, and to those of all ages and experience who enjoy straightforward, uncomplicated study of God's word.

2. Other features of Study Guides

   a) **Layout:** After an introduction and essential background information, the text is examined in more detail. Headings and Bible references make it easy to use the guide for looking up information on any particular section of the Bible.

   b) **Bible versions:** This Guide mainly uses the New King James Version. Other versions are sometimes used where they assist in clarifying a particular passage.

   c) **Manageable sections:** Each Guide is divided into units of study which are not too long. This will make it easier for individuals or groups to make progress. An hour's concentrated and productive study on a regular basis is likely to yield good results.

   d) **Visual help:** Visual help is given wherever possible to increase understanding. The prophets and the Lord Jesus himself used visual illustrations to communicate their message. This should help our understanding of the written word.

   e) **Use alongside the Bible:** The student must have a Bible open alongside the Guide.

   It is recommended that important information is marked in the Bible for future use. Have a pencil ready for this purpose.

   f) **Further study:** The final sections contain suggested answers to the questions raised throughout the Guide, and make recommendations for further reading.

   g) **Prayer:** We are studying the word of God. Before commencing any Bible study we must ask God's blessing on our activity. Thank God for making the Bible available to us, so that through it we may come to know Him and to look forward to His coming kingdom.

   Here is a prayer that sums up these aims:

   "Open my eyes, that I may see wondrous things from Your law."

   (Psalm 119:18)

Preface

NO ONE can read the letter of James without being touched by it. Its message is riveting. He works through issues in our lives that we are aware of, but sometimes prefer to avoid. It might make us feel uncomfortable but it is actually a kindness. Avoiding issues is not good and James is intensely concerned with our eternal well-being. He identifies the things which will hinder us, describes them clearly and tells us what to do about them. What more could we ask? If we can listen to what he says it will change our lives both now and in the age to come.

Not all the passages are easy to understand and I acknowledge a debt to Neville Smart for his book, *The Epistle of James* and to the Tyndale Commentary. These two works have carried more than their fair share of the weight in helping us understand James' message.

I am particularly grateful to John Morris for reviewing the text and making many helpful suggestions. Thanks also to the group of friends who read through the first draft and provided feedback which has resulted in many changes for the better.

The method of this Study Guide is to work though James' teaching as far as possible without interruption to get the full flow of what he is saying. The study points are recorded separately. It is such a practical letter that suggested discussion topics have been included at the end of each section.

The essence of James' message is captured at the end of the first chapter:

"But he who looks into the perfect law of liberty and continues in it, and is not a forgetful hearer but a doer of the work, this one will be blessed in what he does."
(James 1:25)

May we all take to heart the lessons of this wonderful letter.

MIKE LEWIS
BRISTOL
August 2013

Acknowledgments

The publishers express their gratitude for the following:

- Illustrations – Julian Pavett
- Maps – Mark Norris
- Other images & illustrations – Shutterstock.com

Introduction

> **The four New Testament 'James'**
>
> 1 James the Lord's brother (Matthew 13:55). Jesus' brothers were: James, Joses, Simon and Judas. None was included in the group of twelve disciples chosen by the Lord.
>
> 2 James the son of Zebedee and brother of John (Matthew 10:2-4). Prominent among the Twelve we often read of 'Peter, James and John' in the forefront of activities. This James was executed by Herod about AD 44 (Acts 12:2).
>
> 3 James the son of Alphaeus. He is also listed among the Twelve but we hear nothing more about him (Matthew 10:2-4).
>
> 4 James the Less. He was probably given this nickname to distinguish him from the Lord's brother as both had a mother called Mary (Mark 15:40). It is also possible, but not certain, that he was the same as James the son of Alphaeus. We do not hear of him again.
>
> There is also one other James, the father of Judas the disciple (Luke 6:16).

THERE is no doubt that James' letter is among the most practical in the New Testament. He deals directly with how we should live as Jesus' disciples, focusing on a faith so vibrant that it changes a believer's life. It is a challenge to all.

Which James wrote the letter?

There are four men called James in the New Testament (see panel). None is identified specifically as the author of the letter but there is evidence which points in the direction of one of them:

- James the Lord's brother and James, son of Zebedee, were the two most prominent among the four. But James, son of Zebedee, was executed by Herod (Acts 12:2). The James who wrote the letter does not feel bound to identify himself so we can assume he was the Lord's brother. He was the only one who remained and the letter must have been written after James, son of Zebedee's, execution.
- At the Council of Jerusalem James is clearly a leading figure (Acts 15:6-29). This is definitely after the execution so we can safely assume he is the Lord's brother. His leading role is evident: such authority would enable him to write his letter without feeling it necessary to identify himself further.
- Similarities between the communication from the Council of Jerusalem and the letter of James suggest the same author (see panel on page 4).

We make the assumption, then, that James is the Lord's brother. In the end it doesn't particularly matter: whoever the author we accept the letter as God's inspired word.

James' background

The Lord Jesus had a number of brothers and sisters but no brother became one of the twelve disciples (Matthew 10:2-4; 13:55). In time they doubted his work until finally they disowned him altogether in fulfilment of Old Testament prophecy (John 7:2-5; Psalm 69:8). James probably saw Jesus' crucifixion as inevitable since the Lord refused to be deflected from the course he had undertaken. But then James met with his risen Lord (1 Corinthians 15:5-8). We cannot imagine his feelings. He came to accept that here was the Messiah he had looked for all his life, at the same time coming face to face with the brother he thought was dead. His was a deep, personal experience of God's grace. Despite the resistance James had shown, God still wanted him. It must have changed his life and surely impacts his letter. It is a letter inspired by the Holy Spirit but reinforced by personal experience. James asks us to do nothing he has not already done himself.

Who was he writing to?

Although his readers were disciples of the Lord Jesus, the letter was addressed to *"the twelve tribes which are scattered abroad"* suggesting a Jewish focus (1:1). From their earliest days the Jews were divided into twelve tribes. For several centuries before Christ, Jewish communities had formed in many Middle Eastern countries. Known as the Jewish *diaspora*, meaning 'scattered abroad', Jews from these communities travelled yearly to Jerusalem for the festivals required by the Law of Moses. Many were present at Pentecost after Jesus' ascension (Acts 2:5-11). They listened to Peter preaching the gospel and three thousand were baptized. Eventually they returned to their own countries, a process accelerated by the impact of persecution in Jerusalem which scattered disciples (Acts 8:1,4; 11:19). But new converts would not know much about leading the new life in Christ. Support was needed and James had the role of looking

Map showing the Roman provinces and regions of the *diaspora*

INTRODUCTION

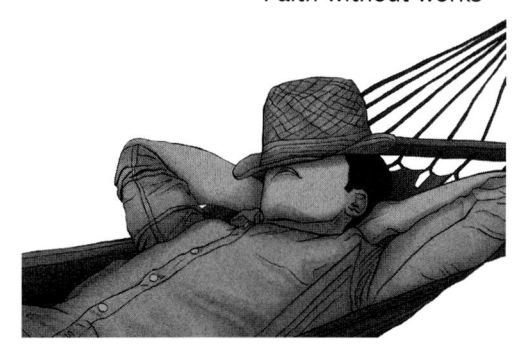

after Jewish disciples (Galatians 2:7-9). So it is a reasonable assumption that he wrote to the scattered Jewish converts to help them grow to spiritual maturity.

The problems James addresses

The background of James' readers suggests two problems needing attention:

- Their orthodox Jewish upbringing emphasised serving God with outward obedience, stressing the letter of the Law.
- They had recently been converted to Christ and rightly believed they were saved by faith. But it appears that some thought faith was all they needed. It was no longer necessary actually to do anything and even outward obedience was a thing of the past. They just had to sit back and wait for the return of Christ. This is a way of thinking James calls *"faith without works"*.

James addresses both problems, teaching his readers that the life of faith means putting the word of God into practice. More than that, believers must allow themselves to receive the implanted word that changes people inwardly, from the heart. The resulting new life is one of active obedience, covering every part of service to God. It is the new life in Christ.

When it was written

The most likely date of writing is AD 43-45, during the early years of preaching the gospel. This was when almost all converts were Jewish. Significantly, James makes no mention of Gentile believers even though he was writing to disciples outside Israel. Neither is there any reference to the Council of Jerusalem which one would expect, and that took place around AD 49.

Features of the letter

Some features of James' letter are particularly worth noting:

- James is grouped with Peter, John and Jude as one of the 'general' letters since they are not addressed to a specific audience like Corinthians or Thessalonians. There are many connections between James and Peter which is no surprise since both were given the commission to work with Jewish converts (Galatians 2:7-9).
- At first the letter seems to be a set of disconnected teachings, but closer inspection shows it is not so random and a flow from one point to the next will be suggested wherever possible.
- A strong Jewish flavour runs through the letter in line with the intended readership. Although James uses the Greek *"ecclesia"* to describe the assemblies of Christ's disciples (5:14), he also calls the assembly a *"synagogue"*, the Jewish meeting place (2:2). Frequent references and allusions to the Old Testament are used, especially Proverbs, which would be easily recognised by his Jewish readers.

And finally …

James' letter is challenging and makes points that many of us might well prefer to

Letter of the law

Faith without works

brush under the carpet. He sets out the life of discipleship in a way we cannot possibly miss. It might sometimes make us feel uncomfortable but we must remember he is doing it because, like his Lord, he wants us to be saved. A fascinating and exciting letter, yes, but be aware: he never lets us off the hook!

Comparison of Acts 15:13-29 and James' letter

Feature	Acts	James
"Greetings" is only used in these two passages (and one other place in the New Testament) in this particular way.	15:23	1:1
Use of "my beloved" or "our beloved" when referring to brethren.	15:25	1:16,19; 2:5
Use of the phrase "name by which you are called".	15:17	2:7
Appeal to his brethren to "listen" to him.	15:13	2:5
The phrase "turn to" or "turn back".	15:19	5:19,20

Justification by faith

NEW Testament teaching on justification by faith underpins James' letter. This section reviews the principles to help us have a better understanding of his message.

Justification: its meaning

Imagine a courtroom scene. God is the judge and each of us is a defendant, accused of sin and facing the death penalty. There's no shortage of evidence against us and we desperately need a way out. We want the judge to acquit us, find us innocent and set us free. Since we are accused of sin and sin means death, our only chance of acquittal is for the judge to declare us righteous. What can we do?

By using this courtroom scenario, Paul, in his letter to the Romans, teaches about faith. He uses the word 'justification' which means bringing a person to a state in which they are considered righteous (see panel). Applied in the legal sense it is used of a judge acquitting the accused and setting them free. How can we get into a position where God finds us righteous and releases us from death?

Justification by works

Our natural inclination is to work so hard at doing the right thing that God is bound to find us righteous. Paul is the ideal person to explain this; he was brought up under the Law of Moses (a detailed law found in Exodus to Deuteronomy). By Paul's time, Jewish teachers had added a lengthy list of man-made rules. These regulations specified how people should live if they wanted to be accepted by God. They encouraged a way of thinking by which rule-keeping conferred righteousness and eternal life. Rather like taking a test: enough ticks in the boxes earned you everlasting life. This is called justification by works. Paul points out that if we were able to earn our salvation this way then God would owe us eternal life as a debt (Romans 4:4).

Justification by works: the problem

Unfortunately this approach won't work. No matter how hard we try we shall always sin at some point. Since *"the wages of sin is death"* we shall always be found guilty no matter how many ticks in the boxes we may have earned. The key point is that even one sin is enough to have us declared guilty (Galatians 3:10; James 2:10). You would need ticks in **all** the boxes **all** the time to earn salvation yourself: you must **never** have sinned. Apart from the Lord Jesus Christ no one has done this, so in the end, no one can justify

---

The meaning of 'justification'

The New Testament is written in Greek and it can help to look at the original meaning of key words like 'justify'. Three related words: *dikaioō*, *dikaiōma* and *dikaiōsis* are frequently used by Paul in his teaching on justification (Romans 2-8, Galatians 2-5). In *Vine's Expository Dictionary of New Testament Words* these are translated with phrases like:

➤ To deem to be right; to show to be right or righteous; to declare to be righteous.

➤ A concrete expression of righteousness.

➤ The act of pronouncing righteous, justification, acquittal.

These help us understand what justification means and what Paul is teaching in these passages.

themselves at the judgement. Justification by works will get us nowhere.

Justification by faith
The way forward is to turn to God, let Him provide a means by which we can be justified, declared righteous and come to everlasting life. This He has done through Jesus' sacrifice, by which our sins are removed and replaced by his righteousness. Salvation is God's gift, not something we can earn ourselves. Salvation comes though belief in God's grace, a grace that led Him to give Jesus for our sins. Justification by faith is this belief and its outcome. Jesus' parable of the Pharisee and the tax collector helps us here (Luke 18:9-14). The Pharisee said, *"God, I thank you that I am not like other men … I fast twice a week; I give tithes of all that I possess …"* This is justification by works. But the tax collector, conscious of his real position, prayed, *"God, be merciful to me a sinner!"* Jesus said: *"I tell you, this man went down to his house **justified** rather than the other."* The tax collector knew he could not save himself and was completely dependent on God's mercy. Justification by faith arises when an individual, recognising their inability to save themselves, turns to God for help. In His mercy God forgives their sins.

The righteous Christ
We are justified, not by anything we ourselves have done, but by belief in God's grace and His gift to us of Christ's righteousness. Think of it this way: our faith in God's grace leads us to baptism when we become part of the body of Christ. We are said to be *"in Christ"*. So when God looks down on us after baptism He sees the Lord Jesus and his righteousness. Before, God saw **our** sins, but when we believe and come to Christ, God sees **his** righteousness. That is why God can justify us, declare us to be righteous and set us free.

Jewish converts: the problem
You can see the problem. Once disciples start living by faith the danger arises that they think nothing more is required of them. It is possible to think that salvation is a matter of just believing, then waiting for Jesus' return. All the evidence suggests that James' readers misunderstood faith to mean they were no longer required actually to **do** anything in God's service. James makes it clear that faith produces lives filled with works pleasing to God. Such works will not **earn** salvation, it is simply that faith **moves** disciples to do them. Jesus' work is to *"purify for himself his own special people, **zealous for good works**"* (Titus 2:14). Faith does not take away the need for godly obedience. On the contrary, Paul says that in Christ we shall lead a new life, pleasing to God (Romans 6).

Conclusion
James gives us the practical outworking of the new life in Christ and shows beyond doubt that a living faith changes lives. Our purpose in studying his letter is to get a better understanding of what this means, to make us *"complete in every good work to do His will, working in you what is well pleasing in His sight, through Jesus Christ, to whom be glory forever and ever. Amen"* (Hebrews 13:21).

Paul and James

Some have seen a contradiction in the teachings of Paul and James, i.e., that Paul emphasises the importance of faith while James teaches the need for works. There is no contradiction. The two apostles are dealing with problems at opposite ends of the spectrum. Paul addresses newly converted Jews, tempted to drift back to the old ways of justification by works (a bit like the Pharisee in the parable of Luke 18). He reminds them that salvation only comes through faith. James on the other hand deals with some at the other extreme; those saying 'faith is all that is needed, that works aren't necessary'. He has to remind them that faith will inevitably show itself in works, in active service to God. It is not that works save, they are simply evidence of a living faith. The difference in approach by Paul and James occurs almost certainly because they were focusing on two different problems arising among early believers.

JUSTIFICATION BY FAITH

A parallel in everyday life

Suppose you live in a village near a wealthy landowner. You agree to work for him each week for a fixed sum and every Friday night you call to receive your wages. Because you have done the work you are entitled to the money: it is cash he owes you as a debt. In the same way, if we were able to keep God's law perfectly we could come to the judgement seat stating we had earned everlasting life. This is what Paul means when he says, *"to him who works, the wages are not counted as grace **but as debt**"* (Romans 4:4).

Suppose, though, you become ill and can't work: you are not entitled to receive anything. But your employer is a generous man and decides to pay you anyway. It is not earned, but a gift. How will you react? Doubtless with gratitude towards your employer, singing his praises. As soon as you recover you will return to work with greater eagerness than before. In the same way, salvation is God's gift of grace. Grace is undeserved favour. Our recognition of that grace is both our salvation and the source of our enthusiasm for serving Him in the new life that inevitably follows.

NOTES

Overview

JAMES clearly uses what he knows about his readers' lives to help them in their spiritual development. In doing that, he provides teaching for believers in all ages. The letter's overriding message is that disciples must be doers of the word. Faith has to show itself in works. Chapter 1 is about how that faith is developed. Chapters 2-5 show how it is then expressed in the new life in Christ.

Chapter 1

Many of James' readers are suffering. Some are poor and oppressed by the rich. All can be persecuted in their Jewish communities for being Jesus' disciples. Rather than become depressed by these difficulties, James urges them to see God's hand at work. The trials of life are God-sent to help them build up faith and develop godly characters. Through answered prayer they learn to trust in God. Nor should they forget that this whole process of growing in faith is dependent on reading God's word and burying its message in their hearts. This in turn should lead to putting the word into practice. Four foundations emerge then, applicable to all believers, on which a vibrant faith is built:

- Recognising God's hand at work in daily life.
- Prayer.
- Receiving the implanted word.
- Doing the word.

The faith that results will lead to a life full of works. At the end of the chapter James gives a thumbnail sketch of what this means which is then expanded in the rest of the letter.

Chapter 2

Divided into two parts, this chapter covers two important principles of daily living. The first principle is love and the second is faith.

Part 1: verses 1-13. Based on the commandment, *"You shall love your neighbour as yourself"* this section is skilfully introduced with an everyday example of discrimination between rich and poor. The real purpose, however, is to emphasise the importance of this great commandment. Not only is it right to live by it now, but it is an essential part of our receiving eternal life at the judgement. We shall need God's grace then, so we in turn show grace to others in this life.

Part 2: verses 14-26. Here James appears to respond to his hearers' objection: 'If we are saved by faith, why do we need to concern ourselves with works? Isn't love a work?' So he gives us what is probably the best known part of his letter. Only a living faith will save when we come to the judgement and that kind of faith will show itself in works now. Works become evidence that faith is alive. James gives three examples of works, covering every part of service to God:

- Concern for others: helping the poor and needy.
- Obedience in our personal life: Abraham offering Isaac.
- Becoming a *"stranger and pilgrim"*: Rahab.

The triumphant conclusion is that at the judgement Abraham and Rahab will produce clear evidence that they had a living faith. It will be their salvation.

Chapter 3

James has established the principles that underpin the new life; he now moves to the specifics. The crux of his message is in chapters 3 and 4. Clearly his readers are troubled by strife and division on a grand scale. He takes us gradually through the causes of the problem and how to resolve it. Chapter 3 focuses on the teacher's role. Teaching has become a vehicle for personal ambition, leading to clashes with other disciples. James highlights control of the tongue as the immediate priority but emphasises that the real solution is letting the heart be shaped by the wisdom which comes from God. Fleshly thinking is self-seeking and leads to confusion; this must not be their driving force. All teachers must aim to be completely unselfish and to create peace among believers.

Chapter 4

Fleshly thinking is further examined here. James calls it double-mindedness since those causing the friction want to be servants of God and friends with the world at the same time. This earthly ambition leads to division. The answer lies in humility and single-minded submission to God's word. James gives three examples of humility in practice, which, like the three works of faith in the previous chapter, cover every part of life. He urges his readers to submit to God's will in:

- Personal obedience: purifying their hearts.
- Relationships with each other: not to judge one another.
- The circumstances of life: future plans must be subject to God's will.

Chapter 5

Essentially this chapter deals with the problem of rich non-believers oppressing poor disciples. James castigates the rich and makes it clear that their downfall is not far away. He urges the disciples to accept their lot with patience, a quality of all God's people. He then deals with the believer's response to everyday life, especially illness, emphasising prayer as being of critical importance. He concludes by reminding them to help fellow disciples who are drifting away from salvation, with that life of faith and works he has so clearly set out in his letter.

Breakdown of the letter

Chapter 1
verse 1	Greeting
verses 2-18	The trials of life
verses 19-27	Our role in the trials

Chapter 2
verses 1-7	Rich and poor
verses 8-13	Love and judgement
verses 14-17	Faith without works
verses 18-20	The debate
verses 21-25	Faith exhibiting works
verse 26	Conclusion

Chapter 3
verses 1,2	Introduction
verses 3-10	The untamed tongue
verses 11,12	The source must be right
verses 13-18	Two wisdoms

Chapter 4
verses 1-5	Strife among believers
verse 6	The basis of acceptance with God
verses 7-16	Humility: three examples
verse 17	Conclusion

Chapter 5
verses 1-12	The rich oppressing the poor
verses 13-18	Prayer and sickness
verses 19,20	Helping disciples who have strayed

3 NOTES

The foundations of faith
CHAPTER 1

Breakdown of the chapter		
Verse 1:	Greeting	AFTER the greeting there are two main sections. (1) verses 2-18 deal with the trials of life; (2) verses 19-27 look at the role we play in responding to the trials. In section 1 James shows how difficulties are God-given to help us develop a mature character (2-4). Wisdom is needed to help us understand what God wants us to learn from our trials. We must not hinder a prayer for wisdom by being double-minded (5-8). Worldly thinking is the main cause of double-mindedness (9-11). Trials make it harder to resist temptation (12-14). The image of childbirth reinforces what James is saying (15-18). In section 2 he focuses on how we work with the trials to become spiritually fruitful. We are to receive the word of God (19-21). And then do it! (22-25). Finally we get a summary of what it means to be doers of the word (26-27).
Verses 2-18:	**The trials of life**	
2-4:	Trials help to develop a mature character.	
5-8:	Prayer for wisdom.	
9-11:	The cause of double-mindedness.	
12-14:	The source of temptation.	
15-18:	The imagery of childbirth.	
Verses 19-27:	**Our role in the trials**	
19-21:	Receive the word of God.	
22-25:	Be doers of the word!	
26,27:	Pure and undefiled religion.	

Verse 1: Greeting
Writing to Jewish disciples scattered round the Middle East James could mention that he is the Lord's brother. Instead he begins humbly, calling himself a **bondservant** of the Lord Jesus. His opening greetings actually contain a message. In the original, *"Greetings"* means 'I wish you joy'. What then, is the joy that James wants them to have?

Verses 2-18: The trials of life

They are to *"count it all joy"* when they are touched by the trials of life. It is probably the last thing they expect. So in this first section James considers the immediate impact of trials in their daily spiritual life. He does not specify here what the trials are, but later we get an insight. Many of his readers are poor which is a problem in itself, but they are also oppressed by the rich (2:6,7; 5:1-8). Add the fact that they are disciples of the Lord Jesus, living in orthodox Jewish communities, and it is clear they have plenty to contend with apart from the day to day pressures of life (5:13,14).

Verses 2-4: The testing of your faith.

James does not pretend that disciples should expect a problem-free existence; he knows that anxieties and burdens come with everyday life. But he urges his readers to see them through eyes of faith: trials are given by God and designed for spiritual growth. They involve a testing of faith since the inevitable human response is, 'Why is this happening? I am trying to serve God and thought I'd be looked after'. They have to recognise that God is looking after them. It is because He wants them to develop spiritually that they

> **Verse 2:** *"trials"* is *peirasmos* which can mean either the difficulties of life, as in this verse, or the temptation to sin as in verse 13. The context must decide.
>
> **Verse 4:** *"perfect"* is *teleios*. It does not mean 'without fault' but 'mature' or 'complete'.

experience the trials. The process of growing under pressure will firstly develop patience, meaning steadfastness; this in turn leads to maturity. But it is vital that through these ordeals they keep the end in view – aiming for a spiritually mature, Christ-like character.

Verses 5-8: Ask in faith.

They need wisdom to understand what God wants them to learn from their trials. Wisdom here means the right frame of mind, a necessary quality if the trials are going to help them develop. If they currently lack wisdom then they must ask God for it; the Father will respond to this prayer because He gives generously and with

> **Verse 5:** *"liberally"* means generous but comes from a word meaning 'single'. It is a contrast with double-mindedness.

a singleness of mind (Matthew 7:7,8). The believer's role is to ask in faith, approaching

---

The law of liberty (1)

The *"law of liberty"* is found in the Law of Moses (Deuteronomy 15). Every seven years Israelites were to remember that, by grace, they had been liberated from Egyptian slavery. They were to demonstrate their remembrance by keeping God's commandment to show mercy to others. The Israelites are a parable for disciples liberated in Christ. By grace, believers have been set free from the slavery of sin and death. James' point is based on Deuteronomy 15:15. Because the Israelites had been set free from Egypt in God's mercy, they were **required** to keep His commandment. The key word in this verse in Deuteronomy is *"therefore"*. In parallel, disciples of the Lord Jesus have been set free by grace and must therefore be *"doers of the word"*. Like the Israelites who had to *"remember"* what God had done for them, James instructs each believer not to be *"a forgetful hearer"* (1:25). To be blessed, both Israelites and believers needed to focus on **doing**. Compare the end of Deuteronomy 15:18 with the end of James 1:25.

THE FOUNDATIONS OF FAITH

The spiritual lightstand

Jesus commanded: *"Let your light so shine before men, that they may see your good works"* (Matthew 5:16). A disciple aspires to be a light in a dark world. The lightstand in the tabernacle was made from one portion of gold, first **hammered** into shape before it could fulfil its purpose (Exodus 37:17). This hammering into shape corresponds to the effect of life's problems on a believer, one who is to be part of the spiritual lightstand which is so much greater (Revelation 1:12,13).

God in the same singleness of mind in which He will respond to them. Double-mindedness shows instability, like a wave tossed by the winds, a restless movement that never makes progress. Double-mindedness is keeping one foot in the worldly camp. It will hinder their prayers and James explores it in the next passage.

Verses 9-11: A flower of the field. These verses, which are really in brackets, look at the cause of double-mindedness. Two mindsets exist: one is concerned with serving God; the other focuses on this present world. Having both is being 'double minded'. Rich and poor can be affected and the problem must be addressed. The poor brother is to forget his lowly status, his envy of the rich who may be proud of their elevated position. The rich will pass away but he is heir to an exalted place in the kingdom in which he can take pride (verse 9). The rich brother is to recognise that his wealth means nothing in

> **Verses 9-11:** in these verses James quotes and interprets Isaiah 40:4-8. The valley is the poor brother and the mountain the rich brother. See also 1 Peter 1:24.
> **Verse 11:** *"pursuits"* means journey and the verb is used in 4:13 as 'will go' where it refers to business trips.

God's sight; it belongs to the world. Scripture shows that his natural life will one day come to an end, like the flower that fleetingly blossoms and fades. A continued focus on life's riches means he will imitate the flower completely and *"fade away in his pursuits"*. That is, he will collapse on a business trip (4:13,14).

Verses 12-14: The crown of life. James returns to the purpose of trials and now goes further by saying these will bring his readers to the kingdom. If they refuse to waver they will receive the crown of life. It is like the crown won by Greek athletes. His readers had observed the athletic determination to be first past the post and James urges them to imitate the same endurance since they pursue a far greater prize (1 Corinthians 9:24-27). But running a race is tiring and this brings James to a problem as relevant

today as it was then: life's problems are hard to cope with. They can make the most resilient person stressed, run down and worn. Temptation becomes difficult to resist. We think we need relaxation and sometimes this means yielding to temptation. But since James has just said that difficulties of life are given by God, does that mean the disciple is being tempted by God? No, if he thinks

> **Verse 13:** the words *"tempt"* and *"tempted"* are *peirazō*, closely associated with *peirasmos* in verse 2, but the context has now changed and they mean a temptation to sin.

like that he is deceiving himself. Temptation comes from the human heart (Mark 7:18-23). This confirms the scriptural principle that no power such as a personal devil is at work when we are tempted. It is the nature we are born with that leads us to sin. God cannot tempt man any more than He can be tempted Himself. He can only give His children good things, designed for their benefit. The trials of life are good; it is the believer's response that can be wrong.

Verses 15-18: Every perfect gift is from above. To aid understanding, James uses the imagery of childbirth. Our natural desires are symbolised by a woman who

> **Verses 15-18:** the imagery is taken from Proverbs 5-9. Our desires are the woman who is 'loose', drawing away her followers to the grave while the woman called 'Wisdom' leads hers to life.

entices us away. When we give in to our instincts we become the father; conception occurs and sin is the child born of desire. Inevitably it grows and the end result is death. But in verse 18 he dramatically reverses the image. God is now the father, the word is His seed, implanted in our natural self. From this conception comes life, the new man in Christ. Any child needs the appropriate conditions to develop if they are to grow to healthy maturity. The new-born in Christ is no exception and the trials of life are part of the right environment. They are the good gifts from the Father to help us develop into the mature characters that please Him.

Verses 19-27: Our role in the trials

In the second section James explains to his readers what they must do to make trials fruitful in their spiritual development.

Verses 19-21: Receive the implanted word. The focus must be on receiving the word of God. James urges his *"beloved brethren"* not to let the pressures of life lead them to be sour and ill-tempered, complaining about anything and everything.

> **No variation or shadow of turning**
>
> God is like the sun which is always the same, it has *"no variation or shadow of turning"* (verse 17). Sometimes we can't see it; instead there are clouds or the darkness of night. But the sun has not gone away. The clouds and the darkness are created by God for our good; they give us rain and allow us to sleep. They correspond to the trials of life. Trials may create darkness for a while but they are for our benefit. Most important of all, like the sun, the Lord God has not left us. On the contrary, the trials are His hand at work in our lives.

THE FOUNDATIONS OF FAITH

> **Verse 21:** reading the Bible is an essential part of developing faith (Romans 10:17).

They should be *"slow to wrath"* and limit the talking, listening instead to the word of God. 'What does the Lord God want me to do? What kind of person does He want me to be? What changes should I make?' More than just listening, it is receiving *"the **implanted** word"*, a key phrase, since it shows how the word is to be buried in the disciple, a seed designed to reproduce itself, as in the image of childbirth. God's word changes the inner self, it produces different people; it is His creative process at work (1 Peter 1:23-2:2; Colossians 3:8-10). But receiving the implanted word is not, by itself, enough. Nothing will happen unless the believer puts the word into practice.

Verses 22-25: Be doers of the word. Here is the theme of James' letter: we must *"be doers of the word"*. He is addressing newly converted Jews who have left justification by works behind. They now believe in justification by faith in the grace of God. Does this mean that works and obedience are no longer necessary? James responds in two ways:

- Even though they are saved by grace, he tells them outright that they still need to keep God's commandments. They must be *"doers of the word"*. Living by faith does not remove this requirement.
- They must look into the *"law of liberty"* and remember what they find. James uses the law of liberty to reinforce and explain his key message (see side panel on page 14). He calls it a 'law' to give it the authority which requires obedience. The lesson he draws is that those who are set free by grace will keep God's commandments (see Romans 8:1,2).

If we remember what we read and put it into practice, our obedience will be blessed; we shall grow and ultimately become part of God's new creation. Even though at times we may not feel we want to *"be doers of the word"* it is an essential part of building a living faith. It changes the inner man, creates a new heart within us, so that as time goes on we shall **want** to be doers of the word. Through faith in God's grace we are set free from death, we have liberty in Christ. But this in turn makes us *"doers of the word"*.

Verses 26,27: Pure and undefiled religion. Finally James provides a summary of what it means to be *"doers of the word"*.

Jesus expressed it in two commandments. Firstly: *"You shall love the LORD your God with all your heart, with all your soul, and with all your mind"*; and secondly: *"You shall love your neighbour as yourself"* (Matthew 22:37, 39). James simply gives practical expression

> **Verse 27:** helping those in need is a reflection of the love God has shown to us: Deuteronomy 10:18,19.

to these commandments. If you love God you will separate yourself from the ungodly aspects of the world around. If you love your neighbour you will control your tongue, you will not spread unkind gossip about them. When you meet those in hardship like widows and orphans, you will see that their needs are met. James is not here defining the whole of religion as we shall see. Indeed, the rest of his letter expands on chapter 1's final verses. He uses these examples to introduce his theme: that we should *"be doers of the word"*.

Conclusion

In chapter 1 James gives four foundations for the life of faith:

1. Seeing God's hand at work in our lives.
2. Prayer.
3. Receiving the implanted word.
4. Doing the word.

In the remaining chapters he expands the last of these; that is, what it means to put the word into practice. It is nevertheless essential that we apply ourselves to all four. The complete life James tells us about in chapter 1 will lead to a new character, created in the inner man. God is at work creating us in His image through the Lord Jesus Christ. We are to be as He intended us in the beginning. We are His children being brought to maturity. Through trials, prayer, reading and doing the word, we become new people. And since the change is from the heart, the works flow in a life that is pleasing to God and gives Him alone the glory. If you want a good summary of what James is saying in this chapter you can do no better than read what Paul wrote in Ephesians 2:8-10. Take a look!

Questions and discussion

Questions

1. What does the word *"Greetings"* mean?
2. Why do we have the trials of life?
3. Where does temptation come from?
4. What is the lesson from the law of liberty?
5. What is the theme of James' letter?

Discussion topics

➤ There are a number of passages in the New Testament which deal with the development of character under trial. They include Romans 5:3,4; 8:28; 2 Corinthians 4:17; Hebrews 12:5-11; 1 Peter 1:6,7. Do they add anything to what James is telling us?

➤ Looking at the last sentence in verse 11 and its expansion in 4:13,14, how do we reconcile a demanding job with discipleship?

➤ What does it mean in practice to keep ourselves unspotted from the world?

The royal law
CHAPTER 2 VERSES 1 TO 13

Breakdown of the chapter
Verses 1-7: Rich and poor
    1-4: Discrimination is wrong.
    5-7: God has chosen the faithful poor.
Verses 8-13: Love and judgement
    8: The royal law: love your neighbour as yourself.
    9-11: Judgement under the Law of Moses.
    12,13: Judgement in Christ.

THERE are two main sections. (1) verses 1-7 deal with discrimination between rich and poor; (2) verses 8-13 draw on this to demonstrate the importance of love with its implications for the judgement. In section one James points out it is wrong for his readers to favour the rich (verses 1-4); God has chosen the faithful poor and the rich oppress them (verses 5-7). In section two he builds on this to highlight the royal law, the commandment to *"love your neighbour as yourself"* (verse 8). By discriminating against the poor, his readers have broken this commandment, with consequences for their judgement. If judged under the Law of Moses they would be condemned (verses 9-11). They need to be judged in Christ where they can receive God's mercy. In turn they must now show mercy and love to those around them (verses 12,13).

Verses 1-7: Rich and poor
It has evidently been reported to James that his readers are favouring the rich at the poor's expense. In this first section he explains why such partiality is wrong.

Verses 1-4: Discrimination is wrong. James paints a graphic picture of a poor, shabbily-dressed man entering the assembly and being told to keep in the background. By contrast, a rich man with his sparkling gold rings and elegant dress is given pride of place. James' readers were giving glory to the rich. But there is only one glory, God's, shown to us in the Lord Jesus Christ, the *"Lord of glory"*. Social differences disappear (1:9-11). He reminds his Jewish readers that discrimination was prohibited under the Law of Moses. Judges were to resist the temptation to show partiality to the rich (Leviticus 19:15). James' readers are succumbing to this temptation, having *"evil thoughts"*. He directs the reader to Leviticus because the law for the judges is underpinned by the great commandment *"you shall love your neighbour as yourself"* and James wants to draw a lesson from it (Leviticus 19:18). But first he has one more point to make.

Verses 5-7: God has chosen the faithful poor. Apparently most of the early disciples, James' readers included, are poor (1 Corinthians 1:26-28). If God has chosen to honour **them** with His salvation, how can they look down on other poor people? Of course it is not all the underprivileged that have been chosen, it is those who love God

> **Verse 1:** *"partiality"* comes from a word meaning 'accepter of a face', that is, a concern with the outward appearance. Sometimes it is translated *"respect of persons"* to capture the teaching although this is not the literal meaning.
>
> **Verse 2:** the word for *"assembly"* means synagogue, the Jewish meeting place. But we know they were disciples of Christ (verse 1).

> **Verse 7:** the *"name by which you are called"* is a special Hebrew expression only used twice in the New Testament, here and again by James (Acts 15:17). It refers to God's possession of His people.
>
> **Verse 7:** an example of blaspheming is the Jews who opposed the gospel (Acts 18:5,6).

and are rich in faith. But the poor are more likely to respond to the gospel because they have nothing else to live for. It reinforces the lesson that we should not seek material things but be happy with the basics of life (1 Timothy 6:6-10). James' readers can see for themselves that the rich around them have a lifestyle that is far from what God wants (James is not referring to rich brothers and sisters here). Such people misuse their power to oppress the poor and to blaspheme.

Verses 8-13: Love and judgement
In section two James returns to the lessons from Leviticus 19 and brings out the reason why discrimination is not right. It is because such prejudice shows lack of love to the poor. Wrong in itself, such an attitude would also impact his readers when they came to the judgement.

Verse 8: The royal law. The commandment, *"You shall love your neighbour as yourself"* appears in both Old and New Testaments (Leviticus 19:18; Matthew 22:36-40). James calls it the royal law because it will be the fundamental law of God's kingdom to which he has just referred (James 2:5). Since it will be the law of the kingdom (because that is how God wants His people to live), we should be living it now. James uses a word for love that is taken from the special Greek word *agapē*. This word is found frequently in the New Testament but hardly anywhere else in Greek literature. It is unlike other Greek words for love such as *philia* which describes a strong bond of affection between family and friends. It is much broader and extends love to include everyone, even our enemies (Matthew 5:44). It is not just an emotion, it is a way of life, a code of living. It is this word which lies at the heart of the commandment which underpins all our relationships with other people. So important is this commandment that James tells his readers they *"do well"* if they keep it.

Verses 9-11: Judgement under the Law of Moses. If believers do not keep this commandment there are implications. James shows that if they favour the rich the law of love has been broken, meaning they have sinned. If they were to be judged under the Law of Moses they would fail to receive

> **Verses 10,11:** to be saved under the Law of Moses it was necessary to keep all of the law without exception (Deuteronomy 27:26; Romans 3:20; Galatians 3:10,11).

eternal life. Under that law, to be saved, every part of it had to be perfectly kept. Since the *"wages of sin is death"*, just one sin would cause a disciple to miss out on eternal life. James uses this fact to highlight the contrast, to show how much they need to be judged in Christ, not the Law of Moses. They require forgiveness of sins, they need to be within the scope of God's love; this He has offered everyone in the Lord Jesus.

Verses 12,13: Judgement in Christ. Clearly, James' readers will not want to come to a **judgement** that takes their sins

So how do we feel about the rich?

James has dealt with prejudice against the poor; it is wholly wrong and has no place in a believer's thinking. Is he saying, then, that we should be prejudiced against the rich? There are those in the world who may encourage such thinking but James is not saying that. God is no respecter of persons, making no distinction between rich and poor when it comes to salvation (Exodus 30:15). It is men and women who discriminate and we must leave human thinking behind. God only divides people into those with, and those without, a living faith. Anyone who comes to Him in faith will be accepted, whatever their social background. The Bible offers numerous examples of rich and poor who had the kind of faith James goes on to talk about. Abraham and Rahab were from opposite ends of the social spectrum but both had faith that brought God's acceptance (Hebrews 11:6).

THE ROYAL LAW

The law of liberty (2)

In chapter 1 James urges his readers to *"look into"* the law of liberty (1:25). Then in chapter 2 they are those who will be *"judged by"* the law of liberty (2:12). There is a progression here which underpins what James is saying. In chapter 1 the law of liberty confirms that believers set free by grace need to obey God's will and be *"doers of the word"*. An Israelite under the law of liberty had been set free from the slavery of Egypt by God's grace: he was **therefore** required to keep God's commandment (Deuteronomy 15:15). In chapter 2 James moves on to the next stage. The commandment the Israelite had to keep was to show mercy to the poor by cancelling debts, giving generously and setting slaves free (Deuteronomy 15:1-14). James applies the same principle to his readers; in Christ they have been freed from sin's slavery and received God's mercy, which they will need at the judgement. But God's grace in liberating them requires that they in turn be obedient to His will by showing mercy and love to others, especially the poor.

Verse 13: those who want to receive mercy will show it to others (Matthew 5:7; 6:12; 7:1,2; 18:21-35; Ephesians 4:32; Colossians 3:13).

into account. Their only hope of salvation is to be in Christ and through God's **mercy** receive forgiveness. Or, as James writes: *"Mercy triumphs over judgement"*. This is being *judged by the law of liberty"* because in Christ, disciples have been liberated from slavery to sin by God's mercy. But salvation is not just something for the future; it affects how we live now. Believers must *"speak and … do"* as those who will be judged in Christ.

Those desiring mercy at the judgement must show it to those around them now, especially the poor. The heart of the matter is belief in the grace of God. True believers are so conscious of God's grace that they reflect it in their dealings with others, to whom they demonstrate that same love they have received from God and want to receive at the judgement. Those not displaying grace to their fellows cannot expect to receive it themselves. If disciples believe from the heart in God's grace, that belief leads to a life which is itself full of grace. Such conviction is a living faith that will reveal itself in works, as James now proceeds to explain – see side panel 'The law of liberty (2)'.

21

Questions and discussion

Questions
1. What kind of meeting place were James' readers using to come together?
2. To what does the phrase *"name by which you are called"* refer?
3. Why is *"love your neighbour as yourself"* called the *"royal"* law?
4. What is the special Greek word for love in the New Testament that James uses?
5. What must we do if we want to receive God's mercy?

Discussion topics
➤ Apart from rich and poor, in what other ways can we discriminate between people and what can we do about it?

➤ If we are to be happy with just having *"food and clothing"* (1 Timothy 6:8), how do we reconcile that with career development? (Luke 12:13-34; 1 Timothy 5:8).

➤ *Agape* means we love everyone. How should we behave towards someone we don't get on with? (Luke 6:27,28; Romans 12:17,18; Ephesians 4:26).

Breakdown of the chapter

Verses 14-17: Faith without works
   14: Faith without works cannot save us.
   15-17: Faith without works is dead!

Verses 18-20: The debate
   18: Surely faith and works are different roles?
   19-20: No: a living faith will always produce works.

Verses 21-25: Faith exhibiting works
   21-24: Abraham: he offered Isaac.
   25: Rahab: she hid the spies.

Verse 26: Conclusion
   26: Faith and works create life.

The living faith
CHAPTER 2 VERSES 14 TO 26

JAMES has made the point that salvation through faith will lead believers to be doers of the word. Above all they will show love to others. He now anticipates an objection from his readers: if we are saved by faith, why concern ourselves with works? We have faith, we know our sins are forgiven, so why not just sit back and wait for the kingdom? Why do we need to do anything? It's this argument that James addresses, with three progressive lines of reasoning: (i) faith without works is dead; (ii) debating the issue and (iii) the living faith will always exhibit works.

Verses 14-17: Faith without works

Here James states his case that a belief that does not show itself in action is no belief at all.

Verse 14: Can faith save him? Faith without works has no value for anyone and certainly has no benefit for the one who holds it. The question, *"What does it profit?"* in this verse alludes to the judgement seat. In the original Greek language, the true meaning is 'Can **that sort of** faith save him?' We are saved by faith but if it is without works, what benefit will that bring us at the judgement? It won't save or give us life; so it is a **dead** faith.

Verses 15-17: Faith without works is dead. Neither does that kind of faith help anyone else. Take the example of aid for the poor. Most have compassionate thoughts towards the needy, considering it important for disciples to provide relief and support. Encountering those in poverty produces sympathy and good wishes: yes, but what are we actually **doing**? That is the question James poses. In what way are the needy actually better off because of what we have done? If the answer is very little, James turns the spotlight on our faith and again asks: *"What does it profit?"* This time the question

---

THERE are three main sections and a conclusion. The three sections are a progression. (1) verses 14-17 emphasise that faith without works is dead; (2) verses 18-20 are a debate about whether this is true; (3) verses 21-25 use Abraham and Rahab to demonstrate triumphantly that a living faith does produce works. In section 1 James says directly that faith without works will not save us (verse 14). Kind thoughts about the poor are useless if we don't do something to help (verses 15-17). Section 2 is an imaginary debate with a challenger arguing the case for faith without works. Aren't faith and works different roles (verse 18)? No, a living faith will always produce works, they are evidence that faith exists (verses 19,20). Section 3 presents an exultant case for faith yielding works with two examples: Abraham, who offered Isaac (verses 21-24) and Rahab, who hid the spies (verse 25). The conclusion is the essential point: only a faith exhibiting works will lead to life (verse 26).

Verses 15,16: helping those in need is an essential part of the life of God's people (Deuteronomy 24:19-21; Isaiah 58:7; Matthew 25:34-36; Acts 2:44,45; 1 John 3:17,18).

has two senses, firstly our faith has not benefited those in need as they are no better off and secondly it will not benefit us at the judgement. In summary, faith on its own, that is, faith without works, is useless; it is dead.

Verses 18-20: The debate

Having stated his case, James moves on to stage an imaginary debate. A challenger argues the case for faith without works and James responds. Paraphrased, the debate goes like this:

> **Challenger:** I have faith and you have works. These are separate roles, rather like one body having different members (1 Corinthians 12:12-31).
>
> **Responder:** OK, but how do you know your faith exists? Without works, what is the evidence for your faith? Where works are present, faith is undeniable, there's real evidence for it. Since we need faith for salvation you're on risky ground here.
>
> **Challenger:** There is no doubt I have faith! I believe the right things; I believe there is only one God, for example, when everyone else worships idols. Since I believe the truth I must have faith.
>
> **Responder:** I know you believe there is only one God and that is good. It is essential to believe the truth. But doctrinal correctness by itself is not enough. The doctrine must change your life. The mentally ill recognised the truth and note: they trembled! At least it provoked

Verse 19: mentally ill people were described in the Gospels as demon-possessed. Often they recognised Jesus for who he really was and were apprehensive (Mark 5:7; Luke 4:41).

Verse 19: the *Shema* is one of the two main Jewish prayers. The first line is, *"Hear O Israel: the LORD our God is one Lord"* (Deuteronomy 6:4). It was the basis of their separation from the idolatrous world around.

A fuller perspective

James has stressed that a living faith will exhibit itself in works. But two things need to be remembered:

➤ Salvation is achieved through belief in God's grace; by this our sins are forgiven. This means that if (hypothetically) someone died immediately after their baptism they would still be saved, even though there had been no opportunity to show their faith in works. As faith grows, works come.

➤ James provides a broad understanding of works. We might think it is just 'doing things', that is practical activities such as aiding the poor. While it does include these, the works arising from a living faith embrace the whole of our service to God. Elderly or infirm disciples, even though not so involved in practical matters, can still show faith in the way they live. Examples of works may include: dealing with difficult people in a Christlike way; choosing a job which will help, not hinder, spiritual life; kindness to staff when in hospital; remembering we are *"strangers and pilgrims"* when buying and furnishing a house; being considerate with neighbours; keeping the tongue constantly in check. There are numerous ways that our faith can show itself and provide evidence that we are disciples of the Lord Jesus Christ.

THE LIVING FAITH

> **Verse 21:** Jesus taught that his disciples must do the works of Abraham (John 8:39).

Paul and James

Both Paul and James quote the same passage regarding Abraham but draw different conclusions (Romans 4:3,9; James 2:23). Paul reasons that Abraham was justified by his faith and James that Abraham was justified by his works. There is no contradiction: Paul and James are dealing with different concerns. Paul is addressing the orthodox Jewish approach, based on the concept that plentiful works earn a place in the kingdom. Paul shows that we are only saved (i.e. justified) by faith. James is dealing with Jews who have left the orthodox approach behind and are committed to salvation by faith. But he takes them to the next stage, expanding on what faith means for daily living. It will inevitably show itself in works; the works become the **evidence** of our faith and in this sense James says we are justified by them. A helpful phrase is *"not by faith only"* (verse 24) which highlights how James was providing an extension to Paul's teaching.

a reaction from them, which is more than can be said for those with faith and no works. Faith without works is dead!

James' message is critical for his readers. If they desire salvation there must be evidence of their faith; works are the evidence. He dramatically sets before them the practical impact of Jesus' parables about the minas, the talents, and the sheep and the goats, all of which have to do with the judgement (Luke 19:11-27; Matthew 25:14-30,31-46). The Lord Jesus is expecting disciples to bring to the judgement some evidence of their faith. He wants to see that his sacrifice has meant so much to them they have changed their lives. This is the full meaning of justification by faith and James is completing the picture begun by Paul in Romans. Though challenging words, they express James' love for his *"beloved brethren"*, because more than anything he wants them to be in the kingdom. His aim is to remove any misunderstanding that could hinder them.

Verses 21-25: Faith exhibiting works

Section three crowns the point of James' argument: a living faith will always produce works. He gives two Old Testament examples, well known to his readers. An important lesson from this section is that works are not just about helping the poor and needy; they have to do with obedience to God's word.

Verses 21-24: Abraham. Abraham believed the promises God made about his future descendants and was justified by this faith (Genesis 15:5,6). The promises would be fulfilled through his son Isaac, yet when Isaac was a young man God asked Abraham to offer his only son as a sacrifice (22:1-19). At the eleventh hour God prevented Abraham from carrying this out, since by his actions he had already proved his obedience. James points to Abraham's willingness to offer Isaac as a 'work' stemming from his faith. James' key phrase is that Abraham's *"faith was working together with his works"*. Real faith and works are inseparable. Abraham was justified by works; not in the sense of **earning** his way to the kingdom or getting ticks in the right boxes. Rather he was justified because he needed faith to be saved and his works showed beyond doubt he had faith; they were conclusive evidence.

Verse 25: Rahab. Abraham was a spiritual giant in the eyes of James' readers. Could they really expect to be like him? James counters their argument by turning to Rahab. A Gentile prostitute, she was entirely different from Abraham. Living in the city of Jericho when Israel were coming to possess the promised land, she hid the

> **Verse 25:** Rahab made a powerful statement of her faith and then took action (Joshua 2:8-16).

Jewish spies sent to the city and aided their escape. Jericho fell to the Israelites but Rahab and her family were saved because of her actions – an example of faith and works at its most simple. Having heard how the God of Israel had delivered His people from Egypt she decided He must be the one true God. This belief changed her life and became her salvation. Like Abraham, her actions were evidence of her faith through which she was justified. Rahab is an example for all disciples; she looked at the world around her (Jericho), decided it was not going to last and joined herself instead to God's people. Through faith she became a 'stranger and pilgrim' and it will be her salvation (Hebrews 11:31,39,40).

Verse 26: Faith and works create life

In the final verse James looks to the creation record. On the physical level, two things are needed for life: a body and a spirit. So too, on the spiritual level, everlasting life needs both faith and works.

Conclusion

James makes his point clearly and conclusively: works are essential. More than that, his definition of works is all-embracing. He indicates three different kinds, each representing a diverse aspect of our service to God:

- Help to the poor and needy (verses 15,16).
- Straightforward obedience to God's will in our individual lives. Abraham's faith shown in works did not involve aid to anyone else at all; it was simply his own personal obedience to God's will (verses 21-24).
- Leaving the world behind and engaging entirely with God's kingdom and purpose. Rahab became a 'stranger and pilgrim' in the present world as soon as she committed herself to helping the spies (verse 25).

James tells us, then, that works stemming from faith are not just helping the poor, but embrace all aspects of our service. They represent the new life in Christ which is where a living faith will take us.

Questions and discussion

Questions

1. What kind of faith is useless?
2. What is the Jewish prayer that states there is only one God?
3. Which people were described in the gospels as demon-possessed?
4. How was Abraham tested?
5. In which city did Rahab live?

Discussion topics

➤ James mentions three different kinds of works. Can you think of examples of these in **our** lives?

➤ James chapter 2 focuses on helping us through the judgement. How does this affect our motives for serving God?

➤ Rahab is used as a worthy example, both in James and Hebrews (11:31). Yet she lied to achieve her purpose (Joshua 2:1-6). How do we reconcile this with the life of faith?

The role of the teacher
CHAPTER 3

Breakdown of the chapter
Verses 1-2: Introduction
   1-2: Don't rush into being a teacher.
Verses 3-10: The untamed tongue
   3-5a: The place of the tongue.
   5b-6: The impact of the tongue.
   7-8: Contrast with the animal world.
   9-10: Blessing and cursing are inconsistent.
Verses 11-12: The source must be right
   11-12: Look to the source.
Verses 13-18: Two wisdoms
   13: Good teaching goes with good conduct.
   14-16: The source of bad teaching and conduct.
   17-18: The source of good teaching and conduct.

THE introduction tells us that James is going to deal with teaching, which is not as easy as some appear to think (verses 1,2). There are then three sections which are a progression. (1) verses 3-10 identify the tongue as the sharp end of the problem – for its size it has immense impact and is untamed; (2) verses 11,12 go further, highlighting that the tongue is only as good as the source driving it, the human heart; (3) verses 13-18 remind us that, in turn, the heart depends on the influence shaping it, either fleshly or godly thinking.

IN chapters 1 and 2 James shows us that faith will lead to a new and different life. Believers become doers of the word and this above all expresses itself in a life based on the law of love. Faith must show itself in works. From these general principles James now moves on to specific actions that need to be taken. Evidently there is conflict and discord among James' readers and the basics of discipleship need revisiting. He uses all of chapters 3 and 4 to deal with this, confirming it is a major issue. This chapter identifies misuse of the teaching role as the source of division and clearly identifies the remedy.

Verses 1,2: Introduction
Teaching comes in many forms: Sunday School, Youth Circle, platform speaking and correspondence work (and all believers are teachers when they talk with those interested in the Bible). There's no shortage of enthusiasm for the work amongst James' readers but he counsels caution. All find it hard to say the right things, including James himself. In a natural progression he identifies the root cause of the problem: the tongue.

Verses 3-10: The untamed tongue
Hard-hitting words in the first chapter have prepared the ground for this section (1:26). The tongue needs restraint. This affects all disciples in terms of spreading gossip, rumour and other kinds of negative speech. But now James applies it specifically to teachers.

Verses 3-5a: Boasts great things. The tongue's influence is out of all proportion to its size and James gives two everyday examples. A tiny bit controls the powerful horse, a small rudder steers a mighty ship. Both illustrate how a little thing sets the course for something much bigger. A teacher gives direction to his hearers. When the tongue is used for self-promotion the direction will be wrong and the result will be significant damage.

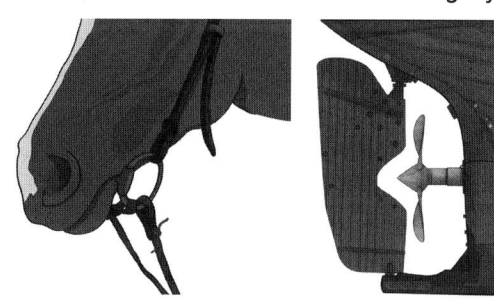

> **Verse 5:** *"boasts"* comes from a word meaning 'to talk big, be arrogant'.

JAMES STUDY GUIDE

Verses 5b,6: The tongue is a fire. Take a forest fire; one tiny spark catches the undergrowth and destroys in hours a forest that has taken years to grow. It is just like a tongue, small but powerful, creating a *"world of iniquity"*. The *"world"* primarily means the person doing the talking: the whole self is defiled by an uncontrolled tongue. More broadly it is everyday life that is affected by the tongue's enormous power. The *"course of nature"* refers to the cycle of life: there's no human activity the tongue can't reach. In turn the tongue is *"set on fire by hell"*. The word for hell is *Gehenna*, the name for the Jerusalem valley where criminals' bodies were burned. It is used here as a symbol of everlasting death and the disobedience which leads to that death. The same disobedience sets the tongue on fire and the tongue then starts an inferno all around it, like the small spark igniting a forest fire.

> **Verse 6:** *"defiles"* is the opposite of *"unspotted"* in 1:27 and James is making the contrast.
>
> **Verse 6:** *"course of nature"* means literally a wheel or cycle. It is a "metaphorical reference to the round of human activity, as a glowing axle would set on fire the whole wooden wheel" (Vine).

Teaching in the New Testament

Without question, teaching was encouraged in the ecclesia; it was both a spirit gift (1 Corinthians 12:28,29) and a role independent of the gifts, where doctrine had first to be learned then taught (1 Timothy 5:17; 2 Timothy 2:2,24-26; Hebrews 5:12). There were two types of teacher, good and bad:

➤ Good teachers. They have the right spirit, that is, humility. They teach gently and in patience. (This does not mean compromising the truth since some may need correcting, in the right spirit of course.) New Testament words associated with good teachers are: peace, faithful, gentle, patient, humility. Such teachers will save their hearers (1 Timothy 4:16; 2 Timothy 2:2,24-26. See also Matthew 23:8-10; 1 Thessalonians 5:13).

➤ Bad teachers. These have two characteristics: firstly they are on an ego-trip and secondly they teach wrong doctrine: both lead to division. Such teachers hanker after status, are driven by pride and like being highly thought of. Words and phrases associated with them are: malicious, fables, disputes, idle talk, envy, strife, useless wranglings, corrupt, destitute of the truth (Matthew 23:5-7; 1 Timothy 1:3-7; 6:3-5; 3 John 10).

James' guidance on teaching in this chapter adds to our understanding of these New Testament principles.

THE ROLE OF THE TEACHER

Verse 7: The four categories of creatures are the same as Genesis 1:26 and 9:2 when man was given dominion over them.

Discussion in the spirit of Christ

Discussions among James' readers are lively to the point of fierce argument. Doubtless those involved think their passionate defence is justified because they stand for a scriptural principle. But their motives are worldly, not spiritual; what they say is harsh and bitter. James is not concerned with the subject of the dispute; instead he focuses on how it is conducted. Bitter arguing is not Christlike and creates division, one of the worst offences (Proverbs 6:16,19). While we should *"contend earnestly for the faith"*, discussion must always be in the spirit of Christ. *"A servant of the LORD must not quarrel but be gentle to all, able to teach, patient, in humility correcting those who are in opposition, if God perhaps will grant them repentance, so that they may know the truth"* (Jude 3; 2 Timothy 2:24-26).

A fire	set on fire by hell	and sets on fire	the course of nature
A world	of iniquity	it defiles	the whole body

Verses 7,8: No man can tame the tongue. At Creation God put the natural world under man's control, so every creature has been tamed. But since man was made in God's image, the tongue was not put under dominion in the same way. No one has completely controlled the tongue (except the Lord Jesus). By nature it is untamed and can do immense damage on the spiritual level, equal to the effect of poison on the physical body.

Verses 9,10: Blessing and cursing. So the disciple needs to have his tongue under control as God originally intended; for James' readers it is only partly tamed. They are using it rightly to praise God, but also for voicing unpleasant things about other people. Since we have just agreed that men and women are made in God's image, something has plainly

Verse 12: The Lord Jesus gives us the same lesson about a tree and its fruit (Matthew 7:15-20). He applied it to false prophets. James does not go that far; he only applies it to bad teaching.

gone wrong. Their behaviour is inconsistent and this has to be put right.

Verses 11,12: The source must be right

So how do we bring the tongue under control? James points to the source. The Lord Jesus identifies it clearly: the human heart or mind (Matthew 15:18,19). The tongue is only as good as the words it is given to speak. By illustration, James provides two examples: water from a spring and fruit from a tree. A spring can produce fresh or salt water but not both. A fig tree will produce figs but not olives; it is the source that counts. Getting the heart right is critical. But James' examples are from God's natural creation; each outcome is fixed. The spiritual creation is not programmed in the same way because men and women

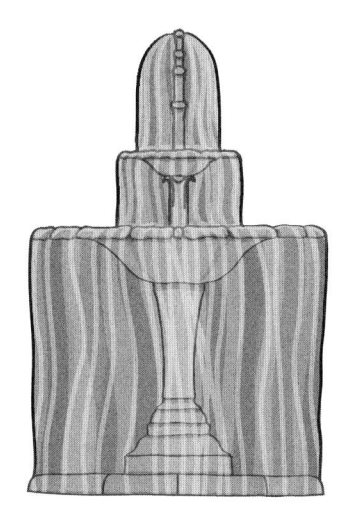

JAMES STUDY GUIDE

> **Verse 14:** *"self-seeking"* is *eritheia*, meaning "seeking to win followers, factions" (Vine). It was used of politicians campaigning for office.

have free will. Each must decide what kind of 'source' they want to be. The Lord God will support us, but we make the decision to allow His word to shape our minds.

Verses 13-18: Two wisdoms

To appreciate how the heart should be, James vividly contrasts good and bad teachers. First he takes the qualities of a good teacher (verse 13), then the bad (verses 14-16) ,and once again the good (verses 17,18). Note the side panel on teaching in the New Testament on page 28: James' words are consistent with those principles and enlarge our understanding.

Verse 13: Wise and understanding. A good teacher shows wisdom and understanding (Proverbs 9:10). A humble acceptance of the Lord God and His word leads to good teaching and conduct. Meekness is recognising one's own worthlessness before God and submitting to His word. It is an emptiness of self, replaced with the things of God. Such a person is both qualified to teach and a blessing to his hearers. A good teacher does not just possess the correct head knowledge but also humility and the lifestyle that results. A good teacher's words will be positive, designed to strengthen, guide and build up in the faith.

Verses 14-16: Self-seeking in your hearts. Lack of humility is the hallmark of the bad teacher. He has head knowledge but has not let go of his natural desires. He is envious, self-seeking and competitive. Such 'wisdom' is not from the scriptures; it is the kind we are born with. When such teachers meet, their self-centred goals conflict: strife, division and factions result. What they say may be correct but their conduct is wrong. Behaviour has as much teaching impact as the spoken word, so bad conduct is the equivalent of teaching false doctrine or lying against the truth (Romans 2:17-24). There can be a number of self-seeking motives for wishing to teach:

- ensuring our view is heard;
- flaunting academic knowledge;
- leading a faction.

Or it may simply be that teachers are perceived to have more status, which is why those with wrong motives are clamouring for the role. The solution to problems of motive is self-honesty, as the Lord God requires in His people (Psalm 51:6).

Verses 17,18: The wisdom from above. Good teachers put their natural desires behind them and receive *"with meekness the implanted word"* (1:21). This wisdom from above gradually changes the heart. James presents a series of qualities that are a progression. Wisdom is **first** *"pure"*, **then** *"peaceable"* and so on through to *"without hypocrisy"*. 'Pure' must come first because a good teacher is honest about himself. These qualities show the **effect** of

Is division ever right?

Let's note that James is dealing with the specific problem of division caused by self-seeking among disciples. He is nowhere suggesting any compromise on belief, i.e., that a group should avoid division even when it is the result of fundamental differences of doctrine. Indeed, elsewhere in the New Testament the command is to separate from those who have turned away from true doctrine. Naturally, everything should be done in a Christlike manner with a view to restoring the one who has moved away (Romans 16:17; 2 Thessalonians 3:14,15; 1 Timothy 6:3-5; Titus 3:10). James wants unity among believers. Such harmony can be shattered both by self-seeking people and differences in belief.

THE ROLE OF THE TEACHER 7

Questions and discussion

Questions
1. What is special about the tongue's influence?
2. What is the *"course of nature"*?
3. When were the four groups of creatures tamed?
4. What controls the tongue and decides what it says?
5. What is the second quality of the wisdom from above?

Discussion topics
➤ Much of James' letter has roots in Proverbs. Look at these passages and think of everyday examples: 10:20; 10:31; 15:4; 17:4; 25:15; 25:23.

➤ Good conduct is one of the qualifications of a good teacher (verse 13). What does good conduct mean for us? See Philippians 1:27,28; 1 Timothy 4:12,13; Hebrews 13:5,6; 1 Peter 3:1-6; 2 Peter 3:11,12.

➤ The qualities in James 3:17 are a progression. In what way does each help to move on to the next? See Romans 5:3,4; James 1:3,4; 2 Peter 1:5-8.

---

wisdom rather than what it is. The striking thing is the total unselfishness of the good teacher; peaceable, gentle, willing to yield … personal interest is sacrificed in the service of Father and hearer alike. There is no place here for ego or pride. Finally James selects peace as the essential quality, confirming that he is dealing with a serious problem of division among his readers. Teachers want to develop the fruit of righteousness in their hearers: the seed must be sown in the fertile environment of peace. And only the truly humble at heart can create peace.

Conclusion
While much of what James says in this chapter applies to all disciples, he is particularly dealing with teachers. It is clear that, under the guise of teaching, negative and divisive things are said about others. His readers have split into factions, each with their own agenda. Speakers use the platform to campaign for their own group while attacking the rest. Here is a lesson for us all. Free discussion about the scriptures is healthy but there is a point where the debate becomes divisive. That point is reached when

groups are more concerned with fighting their own corner than discovering what the Bible says (1 Corinthians 1:10-17). The solution is to be honest about our motives and put into practice James' words about humility and love. The more we can be doers of the word ourselves, the more effective our teaching will be.

Strife – the cause and cure
CHAPTER 4

Breakdown of the chapter
Verses 1-5: Strife among believers
   1-2: Worldly thinking causes strife.
   3: Unanswered prayers.
   4-5: Enmity with God.
Verse 6: The basis of acceptance with God
   6: Grace and humility.
Verses 7-16: Humility – three examples
   7-10: Personal obedience.
   11-12: Attitude to brothers and sisters.
   13-16: Circumstances of life.
Verse 17: Conclusion
   17: Knowledge brings responsibility.

JAMES spends this whole chapter dealing with the cause and cure of strife among believers. He builds on what he has taught so far. The foundations in chapter 1, the love and works of chapter 2 and the role of the teacher in chapter 3 are now focused on a real, practical outcome in the daily life of disciples working together.

Verses 1-5: Strife among believers

Unity is a distant dream for James' readers. Disputes are so intense that they place harmony beyond reach. The first five verses describe the cause of the problem and later James names it: double-mindedness (verse 8).

Verses 1,2: Wars and fights. *"Wars and fights"* arise because James' readers have not rid themselves of worldly desires. It's the wrong kind of war. There is a battle to fight. Every disciple has to combat their own natural instincts; James calls this, the *"war in your members"*. Because his readers are losing this battle they are at war with their brothers and sisters. James does not specifically spell out the connection between

---

JAMES has identified the source of strife as a heart out of tune with God (3:14-16). He now uses the whole of chapter 4 to address this critical issue. There are three main sections and a conclusion. (1) verses 1-5 describe the cause of the problem; (2) verse 6 identifies humility as the cure; (3) verses 7-16 give three examples of humility; (4) verse 17 provides a concluding thought. In section 1, our familiar friend double-mindedness is the cause. His readers love this present world which is the root cause of strife (verses 1,2). It means that prayers are not answered (verse 3). The effect is to make them God's enemies (verses 4,5). Section 2 provides the cure. Disciples should accept God's grace and humble themselves before Him (verse 6). Section 3 provides three examples of humility in practice: obedience in personal life (verses 7-10); attitude towards brothers and sisters (verses 11,12); acceptance of God's overriding guidance in everyday life (verses 13-16). The conclusion is a reminder that knowledge brings responsibility; live what you know to be right (verse 17).

Verse 1: *"wars and fights"* in the Greek have the same meaning which can range from quarrels to physical fighting.
Verse 1: the *"war in your members"* is an echo of Paul's conflict with himself (Romans 7:23). See also 1 Peter 2:11.

the desire for pleasure and the ecclesial conflict, but there are two possible reasons. If teachers work purely for financial gain they will hanker after a monopoly (1 Timothy 6:3-5). Or it might be a race to see who can accumulate the most material goods. The resulting envy leads to strife. Either way, the trouble comes because they still have one foot in the worldly camp. This familiar double-mindedness now takes on a new dimension; discord is getting violent, leading to murder (see panel). It is all so unnecessary; they should go to God in prayer if they need anything.

Verse 3: You ask amiss. We can almost hear the response from James' readers: they are **always** coming to God in prayer. Doubtless they are, but these prayers are dominated by requests to satisfy the flesh; this simply makes the problem worse. Selfish prayers come so easily, yet the Lord Jesus taught that prayer must first be to glorify God. Afterwards we pray for ourselves (Luke 11:2-4). And, whatever we ask for must be 'if God wills' (1 John 5:14). Disciples must be single-minded in prayer; double-mindedness is the greatest hindrance.

> **Verse 3:** *"amiss"* means "whatever is evil in character, base" (Vine).
>
> **Verse 3:** here James repeats the lesson of 1:6-8.

> **Verse 4:** most translations just have *"adulteresses"* which follows the main source manuscripts. The KJV / NKJV add *"adulterers"* based on different manuscripts.
>
> **Verse 5:** *"spirit"* is used in the New Testament to describe a way of thinking or attitude, a state of mind (Matthew 5:3; 26:41).

Verses 4,5: Friends of the world. James uses two illustrations to underline the seriousness of his readers' position.

- Adultery. As the bride of Christ they should be single-minded in their loyalty to him. But the world is attractive and flirting has developed into a relationship.

Was it really murder?

We struggle with the thought that disciples' disputes lead to murder (verse 2). Unhappily this is the most likely interpretation of the word James uses. Some suggest that he means a spiritual death, but this doesn't stand up to examination. Neville Smart wrote about these 'spiritualising' theories: "We must confess to finding them utterly unconvincing; and none of the more reliable commentators on the Epistle has felt able to accept them" (*The Epistle of James*, page 124). The Greek word James uses, *phoneuō*, means to kill, slay or commit murder. New Testament variations of the word appear 29 times and always mean literal killing or murdering, most often when quoting the eighth of the ten commandments, *"You shall not murder"* (Matthew 5:21; James 2:11). Perhaps we can best come to terms with it by recognising that in those days violence was common and life cheap (Acts 14:19).

What would they think if their husbands or wives committed adultery? That is how God feels when they join with the world (2 Corinthians 11:1,2).

- Friendship. If disciples are the world's friend they are God's enemies. James shows in chapter 2 how Abraham was just the opposite: he left the world behind and through a living faith became the friend of God (verse 23).

Spiritual adultery and friendship with the world is the same thing. They stem from the *"spirit that dwelleth in us"* (verse 5, KJV), i.e., the way of thinking we are born with. By nature we hanker for the world's pleasures (see panel). James quotes from scripture but no Old Testament quotation exactly matches his words. He may have in mind a verse associated with the Flood period when people simply gave in to their natural instincts (Genesis 6:5). But the point

Verse 5: the spirit within us

This Study Guide normally quotes the NKJV, but for this phrase we have used the KJV: *"The spirit that dwelleth in us lusteth to envy"*. Spirit here is a worldly way of thinking, a desire for fleshly things. The NKJV and other versions translate it very differently and suggest that James is saying the spirit is from God. It becomes jealous when His people are unfaithful. We have followed the KJV interpretation because:

➤ The key word, *phthonos*, is translated *"jealously"* in the NKJV, but *"envy"* in the KJV. The New Testament use of the word does in fact mean envy of material things; it is not about jealousy in a personal relationship. The meaning of the word is "the feeling of displeasure produced by witnessing or hearing of the advantage or prosperity of others. This evil sense always attaches to this word ..." (Vine). It is often connected with strife, as James uses it here (Galatians 5:26; Philippians 1:15; 1 Timothy 6:4).

➤ It reflects the context of the passage (verses 1-5) where James talks of his readers wanting the things of this world.

➤ The phrase which follows, *"But He gives more grace"*, is a contrast with this fleshly thinking.

The literal translation of the phrase in James is simply: 'to envy yearns the spirit which has dwelt in us'.

is unmistakable: the cause of his readers' problem is double-mindedness, a lingering attachment to the present world.

Verse 6: The basis of acceptance with God

The problem crystallised, James now provides the solution and the chapter turns to exhortation. He starts with *"But"*, indicating that what comes next is in direct contrast with the previous passage. God does not want to be our enemy: He has called us to be His friends, made possible by the grace He has shown in the Lord Jesus Christ. Most important of all, *"He gives more grace"*; the grace is greater than the natural tendency to sin he has just described (verse 5). But it is given only to the humble, confirmed by James' quote from Proverbs (3:34). So what is humility? It is discarding natural desires and submitting to God's will. Double-mindedness disappears with a living faith in God's grace. This new life reveals itself in works – a life lived in humble submission to God's will.

Verses 7-16: Humility – three examples

James helpfully offers three examples of what humility means in practice. Like the works of faith in chapter 2, they cover the broad spectrum of service to God. First he looks at our personal life (verses 7-10), then relationships with each other (verses 11,12) and finally the impact on the circumstances of our lives (verses 13-16).

Verses 7-10: Draw near to God. James begins by putting the believer's personal life under the spotlight. His readers need to make a stand against temptation. He advocates five specific actions, each of which will bring a fruitful result.

The laughter and joy James mentions is not that of the spiritual life. They are not wrong in themselves. His concern is the banter and amusement that comes from indulgence in the worldly life. His readers must let it go if they want to draw closer to God.

Resist the devil	He will flee from you
Draw near to God	He will draw near to you
Cleanse your hands	You stop sinning
Purify your hearts	You become single-minded
Humble yourselves before God	He will exalt you

Verses 11,12: One lawgiver. Next an examination of the relationship of James' readers with each other. Pride puts them on a pedestal, elevated over their brothers and sisters. They criticize and judge, which is wrong in itself. But the problem goes further. Each time they judge they ignore the law, *"You shall love your neighbour as yourself"*. By discounting it, they state that this law is not right; otherwise they would keep it. They

Verse 13: there was a great deal of commercial travelling in the first century (Acts 16:14).

Verse 14: parallels the rich man and his barns (Luke 12:16-21).

Verse 15: we must recognise that God is in control of our lives (Acts 18:21; 1 Corinthians 16:7).

STRIFE – THE CAUSE AND CURE

are like the man who *"speaks evil of the law and judges the law"*. His pedestal takes him so high he is above the law itself. Such a disciple is no longer one who **does** the law but one who has become a judge, a lawgiver; someone who **creates** the law. But there is only one lawgiver, the Lord God, so he makes himself equal with Him. It is astounding how far natural instinct takes those who lack humility. But remember, James says, not only does the Lord God make the law, He holds the power to show grace in saving men and women. His readers do well then to humble themselves before Him and accept His law to love one another. They have received God's grace and forgiveness; they should show the same to others. This will remove strife and bring unity to Christ's body (Ephesians 4:31,32).

Verses 13-16: What is your life?
Finally James turns to the circumstances of daily life. His readers want worldly things, but they cost money. The result is an intense focus on work, especially for those with their own business. Commerce means travel and their enthusiasm for generating wealth is captured in the detailed planning of the proposed business trip (verse 13). It is pride twice over, *"you **boast** in your **arrogance**"*. They need to recognise that their lives are in God's hands and could end tomorrow. That alone should bring them to concentrate on serving Him. A humble acceptance of His power over their lives promotes single-minded service. And it brings the disciple into oneness of mind with brothers and sisters, removing the competitiveness that comes from a world-centred focus. We must take the lesson to heart. We need to earn our living which will always require planning. But such plans must be *"if the Lord wills"*. The reminder of life's fragility will help keep our priorities right. Our Lord left us in no doubt what these should be: *"seek the kingdom of God, and all these things shall be added to you"* (Luke 12:31).

Verse 17: Conclusion
James has identified both the cause of the strife and its cure. Double-mindedness, wanting to serve God **and** Mammon, is the cause. Accepting God as supreme is the cure. Genuine humility will unite his readers and remove the discord infecting their fellowship. Are they free to accept James' teaching only if they feel like it? No, they know what it means to **do** the right thing; they must act on it. They must **do** the word; their faith must show itself in works.

Questions and discussion

Questions
1. What is the *"war in your members"*?
2. What should come first in our prayers?
3. How did Abraham become the friend of God?
4. What do we bear in mind when planning the future?
5. What is the impact of knowing the right thing to do?

Discussion topics
- How can the lessons about friendship we learn in everyday life be applied to spiritual friendship with God and the Lord Jesus?
- What does it mean in practice to *"resist the devil"*, *"cleanse your hands"* and *"purify your hearts"*?
- In what ways can God's will affect our future plans?

NOTES

Patience and prayer
CHAPTER 5

Breakdown of the chapter

Verses 1-12: The rich oppressing the poor

    1-6: The rich are about to be judged.

    7-12: Disciples must learn patience.

Verses 13-18: Prayer and sickness

    13: Let him pray.

    14-15: The act of healing.

    16-18: The importance of prayer.

Verses 19-20: Helping disciples who have strayed

THERE are three sections in this chapter. Section 1 verses 1-12 deal with the rich oppressing the poor; section 2 verses 13-18 look at prayer and sickness; section 3 verses 19-20 encourage readers to help those drifting away. Section 1 tells of wealthy Jews oppressing poor disciples. But they are soon to be judged (verses 1-6). James then turns to the disciples on the receiving end, asking them to develop patience, especially in waiting for Jesus' second coming (verses 7-12). Section 2 urges a spiritual response to life's conditions and then focuses on healing (verses 13-15). From this James develops the theme of prayer, using Elijah as an example (verses 16-18). Section 3 identifies the need to help the fellow disciple who is losing faith (verses 19-20).

Verses 1-12: The rich oppressing the poor

Section one focuses on the rich oppressing poor disciples. Almost certainly these rich are the same ones dragging James' readers to court (2:6,7). They are non-believers and probably wealthy Jews, suggested by the inferred Old Testament references. As they are not among his readers, James writes them an imaginary letter (verses 1-6) before urging disciples to be patient (verses 7-12).

Verses 1-3: Miseries coming upon you! The rich are about to be judged. Some years after this letter was written the Romans destroyed Jerusalem (AD 70), leading to a widespread persecution of the Jews. It was God's judgement for their persistent disobedience that culminated in the crucifixion of the Lord Jesus (Matthew 21:33-41; Luke 21:20-24). James paints a vivid picture: costly clothes are moth-eaten because the wearers are no longer there to use them; he sees a strongroom full of carefully stored cash, corroded through lack of use. Money should not be stored in the first place but used to help the poor. Corrosion is therefore a witness against the accused, a symbol of the fire about to consume them. It was folly; these rich men live in the last days of Moses' covenant. With less concern about worldly wealth they could come to Christ and lay up treasure in heaven.

Verses 4-6: You have fattened your hearts. From a general picture of future judgement, James focuses on three specific sins committed by the rich.

- Verse 4 – Workers in the fields are defrauded of their wages. This is contrary to the Law of Moses as the rich probably know (Deuteronomy 24:14,15). But God has heard the labourers' cries.
- Verse 5 – The rich live in unacceptable luxury, ignoring the needy. They do this *"on the earth"*; a reminder that they should be laying up heavenly treasure.

> **Verse 1:** *"howl"* is an Old Testament word used when God's judgements are about to appear (Isaiah 15:3).

> **Verse 4:** *"Sabaoth"* means "hosts" and comes straight from the Hebrew Old Testament. It is used in *"LORD of hosts"*, often in connection with judgement (Isaiah 6:3,11,12).

> **Verse 6:** *"condemned"* is a legal word, confirming they were going to court.

It is leading them to judgement like fattened cattle to slaughter.
- Verse 6 – In oppressing poor disciples, the rich take them to court to have them condemned and killed. But disciples have followed Jesus' teaching of non-resistance.

There's no question of how unjust the rich are towards God's people. They should know better: they have His law in their hands.

Verses 7-9: You also be patient. Now James provides encouragement to disciples suffering under these oppressors. He does it by taking their minds from life's troubles and directing them towards Jesus' second coming. Waiting for this wonderful event develops patience, an essential quality in God's people and part of the training for those who would be in the kingdom (1:2-4). Farmers are patient as they wait for rain, learning on the practical level what believers learn on the spiritual. In God's creation everything has its time. No one knows when Jesus will return. James – like the Apostle Paul (Philippians 4:5) – says the coming is *"at hand"* but that is because it is **possible** and therefore his readers must live as if they know his coming is soon. The pressures they suffer must not cause them to grumble about fellow disciples. The possible nearness of the Lord means the judgement may be imminent. James has told them to show mercy to others if they want a merciful judgement themselves (1:12,13). So, no grumbling or criticism!

> **Verse 8:** *"establish"* means to place firmly, set fast, to fix.
>
> **Verse 9:** The judgement here clearly refers to all disciples, that is at Jesus' second coming. It is not the specific judgement on the Jews in AD 70 referred to in verses 1-3.

Verses 10,11: We count them blessed who endure. To help our understanding of patience, James gives Old Testament examples: the prophets and Job. God requires two qualities in His people and life's trials are there to help develop them. The first is **patience, in the sense of longsuffering**, and the second is **steadfastness, meaning perseverance**. For the first, James directs his readers to the prophets who spoke *"in the name of the Lord"*. They suffered for this, persecuted by fellow Jews who were doubtless among the rich (Matthew 5:12). But though they spoke God's word, upholding it vigorously, the prophets never defended themselves. For the second quality James points to Job as a model of steadfastness under trial. He did not hesitate to vocalise his confusion but was always wholly loyal to God. There was no shortage of reasons for him to give up but he persevered. Finally he learned that the Lord is compassionate and merciful (Job 42:10-17).

Verse 12: Let your 'Yes' be 'Yes'. Living under pressure creates stress and

PATIENCE AND PRAYER

that can produce behaviour that is anything but patient. James identifies swearing as an example; not swearing in the sense of bad language but the taking of oaths, an emotional over-statement designed to emphasise a point. James almost quotes the words of the Lord Jesus (Matthew 5:34-37). The way to get people to believe them is to earn a reputation for meaning what they say!

Verses 13-18: Prayer and sickness

Section two of the chapter is divided into three parts: the first is about responding to God in daily life (verse 13), the second is an act of healing (verses 14,15) and the third

> **Verse 13:** *"psalms"* refers to singing praises generally, not just Old Testament psalms.

The gift of healing

It is the prayer of faith that saves the sick and we must all pray for those who are ill. But in this case James must have had more than prayer in mind or it would not be necessary for the elders to be present. Prayer can be carried out at a distance. Looking at the Spirit gift of healing in the New Testament we find that four things were involved:

1. Prayer (Acts 28:8).
2. Anointing with oil (Mark 6:13).
3. The miracle was carried out *"in the name of Jesus Christ"* (Acts 3:6).
4. The laying on of hands (Mark 16:17,18).

The first three are included in James' instructions. Possibly the fourth is part of the process also, if that is what James means by the unusual phrase, *"pray over him"*. The original word for *"over"* has a number of meanings including 'upon'. Oil was also used as a medical treatment (Luke 10:34) but that is unlikely to apply because, again, it would not be necessary to call the elders. The anointing with oil is not explained in the New Testament but indicates the healing was God's work (Leviticus 8:10-12). We conclude that James refers to the use of the Spirit gift of healing, probably possessed by at least one of the elders from this first generation of believers.

draws out the importance of prayer (verses 16-18).

Verse 13: Let him pray. Expressing our emotional state in words comes naturally. James has just counselled his readers to avoid grumbling when stressed but he does not expect them to bottle up tension. Instead he tells them to direct their feelings Godwards. When suffering, pray; if happy, sing

> **Verse 14:** elders and bishops are two different Greek words but they are used interchangeably in the New Testament.

God's praises. This provides release in an acceptable way to God.

Verses 14,15: The act of healing. Then he pinpoints one frequent source of stress: sickness. When we hear of someone we know who is ill we should come to the Father in prayer and place them in His hands. He is all powerful and can heal them if it is His will. The healing described here is the result of a Spirit gift, possessed by some first-century believers (see panel on page 41). With physical healing comes the forgiveness of any sins relating to the sickness. There is a general connection between sin and sickness arising from the curse. But in some cases there can also be a specific connection (Mark 2:1-12; John 5:14). Clearly it does not always apply because James uses the word *"if"*. It is certainly not something we can apply to others when they are sick! James helps us

> **Verse 16:** *"fervent"* is the Greek *energeō* from which we get the word energetic. It helps us understand what James is saying.

deal with it because the context concerns approaching God in prayer. So, if we are unwell, rather than worrying overmuch about whether the illness relates to a specific sin, we must come to the Father. We need to ask for the forgiveness of **all** our sins and for the healing of our illness. We can be sure of the first, but the second will depend on His will for us. Prayer provides the link with the next section.

Verses 16-18: The importance of prayer. Disciples should declare their faults to each other; then they can pray for one another, *"that you may be healed"*. Whether the healing relates to a physical condition or spiritual healing (i.e., the forgiveness of sins) is not clear. The second is the most likely as there is no suggestion of physical illness in this passage and the prayers relate to spiritual trespasses. Either way the prayer must be fervent. James' example is Elijah. Though scripture is silent, we can safely assume Elijah did pray and James confirms it (1 Kings 17:1; 18:42-45). Unquestionably, Elijah was fervent: he looked for rain seven times. James says the drought lasted three and a half years, though 1 Kings 18:1 tells us that the rain returned *"in the third year"*. It does not say, however, that the *third year* relates to the drought; it may refer to

PATIENCE AND PRAYER

Questions and discussion

Questions
1. What was the judgement about to come on the rich men?
2. Who were examples of patience from the Old Testament?
3. What should a disciple do when suffering?
4. What is one quality a prayer should have?
5. What do you achieve if you bring back someone who is leaving the faith?

Discussion topics
➤ What are the modern equivalents of disciples being oppressed and how should we react?
➤ What specific examples are there of the prophets and Job showing patience?
➤ In what ways can we put verse 16 into practice?

something else. The accounts of the Lord Jesus and James agree on this (Luke 4:25).

Verses 19,20: Helping disciples who have strayed

The final section deals with saving a fellow disciple and the letter closes on the theme of helping each other (verses 19,20). If someone's spiritual problems are so great that they are leaving the faith, then no effort must be spared to bring them back. It will *"save a soul from death"* and covers a multitude of sins. Whose sins are these: the person being saved or the one doing the saving? The most probable answer is that the sins covered belong to the one falling away. Context suggests this and the phrase *"save a soul from death"* parallels *"cover a multitude of sins"*.

NOTES

Do good to all

> The letter of James is often referred to as the main source of teaching about good works. It is helpful to see how it fits into New Testament teaching as a whole. In this section we look at New Testament guidance about discipleship and good works.

ONE of the most well known passages in James is his teaching that faith must show itself in works. When we looked at this passage, we discovered that he gives us three examples of works which together cover the whole life of the disciple:

- Helping those in need.
- Obedience to God's will in our personal lives like Abraham.
- Becoming *"strangers and pilgrims"* like Rahab.

The first of these can give rise to many questions, especially for disciples who live in parts of the world where they have resources to spare which can be used in the Master's service. How do we divide our giving between preaching work and helping those in need? Should we contribute to charities in the world around or just support our fellow disciples? The purpose of this section is to explore New Testament teaching about good works to see if we can find some answers to these and similar questions. For convenience the phrase *"good works"* is used in this section to refer to help for those in need. We must remember however that the term *"good works"* is normally used in the much wider sense of describing the whole life of discipleship.

Firstly we shall look at the scriptural principles, then at the New Testament passages which relate to good works, and finally we shall address some questions on this subject that are often raised.

Eternal life comes first

Love in action will express itself first in preaching the gospel. People in the world are dying and disciples have the gospel which will bring them to everlasting life in the kingdom of God. This must always be the priority and govern our dealings with others. The Lord Jesus made this abundantly clear in the miracle of the feeding of the five thousand. It began with Jesus spending most of the day teaching the multitude which had followed Him. When they were tired and hungry He provided for them through the miracle of the loaves and fishes. Excited by the prospect of endless supplies of food, the crowd decided to make him king. But the Lord refused, clearly setting out the priorities: *"Do not labour for the food which perishes, but for the food which endures to everlasting life …"* (John 6:26-29). The reason is simple: physical food provides for this life only; spiritual food leads to **eternal** life (Matthew 4:4; John 4:13,14; John 6:48-50,58; Acts 6:1-4). The first principle then, is that spiritual food is the priority.

The Lord's example

Consistent with this we find a second principle at work in the lives of the Lord Jesus and the apostles. Preaching the gospel came first. As they carried out this work they helped those they met who were in need, but they did not set out to find them. We are told that the Lord Jesus travelled round Israel taking the good news of the kingdom of God and healing the sick (Matthew 4:23). But when just one of those two is selected, it is the first (Mark 1:14,15). This prioritising is reflected throughout the gospels. Our Lord focused on preaching and teaching. In doing this he inevitably encountered people with problems who he was able to help, but he did not seek them out. The apostles too spent their lives in taking the gospel to the world, and in doing this they clearly helped those they met along the way who were struggling (Acts 3:1-10). This approach is captured in the parable of the Good Samaritan. Here was a man who was simply going about his daily life, possibly on a business trip. Seeing someone in trouble he helped as best he could. But his caring was part of his everyday life; he had not set out to find someone in need (Luke 10:30-37).

Not putting the world right

The problem of suffering existed in the time of the Lord Jesus and it exists today. During his earthly ministry, however, Jesus did not attempt to right the world by removing all its problems. Although he *"went about doing good"*, it is clear he did not remove all the distress that he met. There must have been occasions when he encountered, say, a leper camp, knowing full well he could cure all its occupants with a word, but turned and walked away. The world was as full of suffering at the end of Jesus' ministry as it was when his work began. Indeed, the Lord said: *"You have the poor with you always"* (Mark 14:7). Does this mean Jesus failed in his mission? No, his purpose was not to solve the world's problems at his first coming. Rather it was to address the source of **all** the troubles of this age, that is, sin. In conquering sin Jesus was completely successful and triumphed over it on the cross. When he comes again sin will be permanently eradicated and with it will go the problems of this present life. A disciples' prime role now is to preach the good news of the Master's victory over sin and the coming kingdom of God, when the fruits of this triumph will finally flourish. This gives us the third principle: our role is not to put the world right. On life's path we shall see many in need and will help where we can, but 'help' is all it can be. The permanent solution will unfold when the Lord Jesus returns (Psalm 72:1-4,12-14).

"Do not do your charitable deeds before men"

Just after he explains what it means to love our neighbour, Jesus warns his disciples about the dangers of giving in public. Using the hypocrites in the synagogue as an example, he spotlights the natural human desire to *"have glory from men"*. So he counsels: *"Take heed that you do not do your charitable deeds before men."* His teaching is strongly worded, including *"… do not let your left hand know what your right hand is*

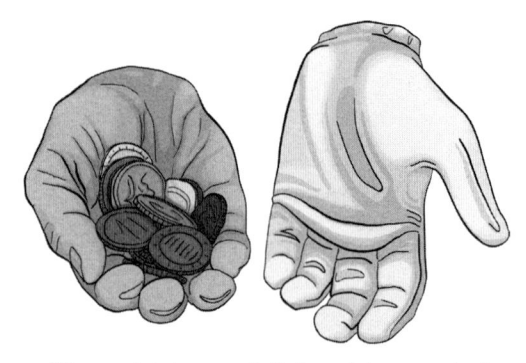

"Do not let your left hand know what your right hand is doing"

DO GOOD TO ALL

doing" (Matthew 6:1-4). Our fourth principle then is that we should aim to make our giving as discreet as possible.

The importance of good works

With these priorities and within this overall framework it is clear that good works are an essential part of a disciple's life, and we shall now briefly review New Testament teaching. A good starting point is Paul's advice to the Galatians: *"Do good to all, especially to those who are of the household of faith"* (6:10). We shall look first at *"Do good to all"* and secondly at *"the household of faith"*.

Do good to all

The gospels. Nowhere is love expressed in works more clearly than in the life and teaching of the Lord Jesus:

- There are numerous examples of the Master's concern for those who suffer and of his practical expression of healing and support. Almost every kind of human illness, physical and mental, was cured by our Lord: lepers, the blind, the mute, the paralytic and the deaf. Jesus taught us to give alms to the poor, food to the hungry, water to the thirsty and a spare coat to the person without one. Loving our neighbour means giving to all who ask and extends even to our enemies. Help is not just for friends in need but those we may not particularly get on with.

- If one passage illustrates both the Master's teaching and example, it is the parable of the Good Samaritan already mentioned. Here was a completely selfless man, concerned only with his neighbour's problems. Nothing was too much trouble either in work or expense. Like the Lord, he had compassion on the man, a response that produced immediate, practical expression.

Acts of the Apostles. There are some helpful passages in the Acts of the Apostles:

- The healing of the lame man is one of the earliest incidents recorded (Acts 3:1-10). Like many of the New Testament miracles it was designed to support the preaching of the gospel but was also an act of compassion by Peter and John (Acts 4:8-12). It was followed by many other examples of healing during the course of their preaching (Acts 5:12-16; 9:36-40; 14:8-10; 19:11,12; 20:9,10).

- Cornelius is described as a *"devout man"* and one of the qualities highlighted is that he *"gave alms generously to the people"* (Acts 10:1,2).

- Note Paul's words to the Ephesian elders: *"I have shown you in every way, by labouring like this, that you must support the weak. And remember the words of the Lord Jesus, that he said, 'It is more blessed to give than to receive'"* (Acts 20:35).

Letters to the ecclesias. Here is the same clear teaching about love in action:

- Preaching comes first; helping the poor accompanies preaching. James, Peter and John encouraged Paul and Barnabas in their mission to preach to

---

The spirit of Christ

The love so clearly defined in scripture is based on the teaching *"whatever you want men to do to you, do also to them"* (Matthew 7:12). A disciple identifies with another's need and does something about it; an unreserved, uninhibited, unquestioning love in action. So when we see someone with a problem, whether spiritual or material, our first reaction must be to help. It may be that our second response is to apply the brakes a little. Sometimes it is simply unwise to give or we just don't have adequate means to help. But our response should always be in this order: wanting to give first and having reservations second. It is possible to have an opposite mindset: to find reasons not to give first and then relent perhaps reluctantly. This is not the spirit of Christ. If we allow the word to develop in us the heart and mind of our Master, then we shall always react to another's need with a heartfelt sympathy and a desire to do what we can. Only then should any secondary considerations arise.

47

the Gentiles. Paul relates that, *"They desired only that we should remember the poor, the very thing which I also was eager to do"* (Galatians 2:9,10).

- Later Paul highlights the need for perseverance, urging: *"Let us not grow weary while doing good, for in due season we shall reap if we do not lose heart. Therefore, as we have opportunity, let us do good to all"* (Galatians 6:9,10).
- Sometimes giving can create problems. Paul deals with this when he advises Timothy on caring for widows (1 Timothy 5:3-16). Our experience of mission work in poorer areas of the world confirms the wisdom of being careful when it comes to giving money. Jealousies can arise among those who have not received any gifts and encourage doubtful motives for attending meetings among those who have.
- Rich disciples should share their wealth with the needy. There is a levelling, an equality which we have already seen in James (1 Timothy 6:18; James 1:9-11). Finally in the letters we find a simple declaration in Hebrews: *"But do not forget to do good and to share, for with such sacrifices God is well pleased"* (Hebrews 13:16).

Revelation. One of the most powerful passages in the New Testament is the Lord Jesus' message to the Ephesian ecclesia, telling them that although they have firmly maintained the true doctrine they have left their *"first love"* (Revelation 2:1-7). This is not about commitment to doctrine (he has just commended them for that), but love here is the Greek *agapē*, meaning love of one's fellow man. Jesus urges them to return to their *"first works"*; that *"love for all the saints"* Paul found in Ephesus years before (Ephesians 1:15). This is consistent with James' teaching that just believing the right things is not enough. Belief must show itself in works.

Especially the household of faith

Let's complete the quotation from Galatians. Paul said, *"Let us do good to all, especially to those who are of the household of faith"* (6:10). The emphasis here needs to be taken into account. While, as already seen, believers assist all in need, they are to give priority to fellow disciples. Concern for the household runs through the New Testament.

- The Lord gives a remarkable list in his discourse on the judgement. Disciples who are saved will have provided food, drink, hospitality, clothing and will have visited the sick and prisoners. He discloses who these recipients are: *"You did it to one of the least of **these my brethren**"*, that is, the household of faith (Matthew 25:31-40).
- Concern is evident in the sharing of material goods to make sure no one lacked (Acts 2:44,45; 4:32-34) and in the daily distribution of food to the widows (Acts 6:1-3).

Justification by works

It is easy to fall into the trap of thinking that we earn our way to the kingdom. Today's world functions on the basis that if you want rewards you must work for and earn them. Once you have done this you are then **entitled** to the reward. Scriptural truth is very different from human thinking. Everlasting life is the gift of God, an expression of His grace. What the Father wants is our trust in His grace and for this belief to develop into a living faith that shows itself in our lives. Our role is to forget self, build up faith and let the good works flow.

DO GOOD TO ALL 10

- Paul urges the Corinthians to provide funds for their poorer brothers and sisters in Jerusalem. Above all, the help had to be given willingly, out of love, for *"God loves a cheerful giver"*. Giving is a hallmark of obedience to the gospel. (1 Corinthians 16:1-4, 2 Corinthians 8 and 9).

- Peter describes us as stewards of our worldly wealth. If we are good custodians we will share it with our brothers and sisters according to need (1 Peter 4:10). John tells us that true disciples have the love of God abiding in them, which shows itself in helping fellow disciples (1 John 3:16-19).

Summary

From this brief review of New Testament teaching we see that the practical expression of loving our neighbour is governed by four main principles:

1. Our priority is preaching the gospel and providing for everyone the spiritual help that leads to salvation.

2. As we go through life we shall come across those with practical needs. We do what we can to help, especially where it concerns our brothers and sisters.

3. It is not our mission to remove the world's problems; that will happen when the kingdom comes.

4. We should not publicise our charitable works.

With these principles in mind we suggest some answers to frequently asked questions on this subject.

1. Should we contribute to non-Christadelphian charities?

- The first answer is yes. One lesson from the Good Samaritan is that we make no distinction when helping those in need. Jesus clearly taught that we should do good to all, even those who are not our friends (Matthew 5:43-47). Clearly we need to avoid charities with political or religious objectives.

- The second answer is that we should keep in mind the brotherhood's charitable funds which are designed to help those in need.

- The third answer is to remember the priorities Paul gave to the Galatians: *"Let us do good to all, especially to those who are of the household of faith"* (Galatians 6:10). As we have seen, there are many New Testament passages about helping our brothers and sisters.

2. Should we work for a charity?

This is very much a matter of conscience. If a brother or sister is moved to express their love for others in full-time work then it is right that they should. Again we need to avoid working for an organisation with political, humanist or religious aims.

3. How do we resolve the conflict of allocating our limited resources of time

49

and money between the spiritual and the material?

Scripture emphasises the spiritual as the primary focus for our energies (John 6:27,48-50,58). Jesus' disciples are to preach, to save men and women, to bring them to everlasting life to the glory of God. As they do this disciples will encounter 'want' in all its forms: hunger, sickness, loneliness or any of the ills of this present world. Moved with compassion they will take action to alleviate the suffering. But Jesus' priorities are clear.

4. It is sometimes said that we should focus on good works because 'good works are what it's all about'. Is this right?

The emphasis with this approach is different from that given us by the Lord Jesus as we have seen. For him, the focus for love in action was preaching the gospel. We also need to remember the path that leads to good works. Through faith we are being recreated in God's image. Since God is love, then as we are renewed in heart and mind we shall develop the love that shows itself in works. But it is essential that we follow this path. In our enthusiasm for good works there is a risk that we can bypass faith and the development of godly love. Then we have only the works and we cannot be justified by these alone (see panel on page 48). The New Testament warns us against this way of thinking. It is possible for someone to lead a life full of good works but have no love at all and miss out on salvation (1 Corinthians 13:3). James tells us that faith must lead to works but the opposite is also true, that is, the works must arise from faith and love (see Ephesians 2:8-10, Colossians 3:10).

5. Does James' teaching about helping the needy mean we should do less Bible Study and concentrate more on good works?

When reading James we can be tempted to go straight to the passage in chapter 2 about good works. But before reaching these verses James has taught us to *"receive with meekness the implanted word"* (1:21). Bible study is an essential part of developing faith and ensuring we are *"thoroughly equipped for every good work"* (Romans 10:17; 2 Timothy 3:16,17). Indeed the whole of James' first chapter is about building up a living faith which will result in the good works he goes on to describe. The *"implanted word"* is the seed of God buried within us and, like any seed, it is designed to reproduce itself. Our Bible Study, together with the other things James writes about in chapter 1, is the means by which our faith and love are developed and by which we are recreated in God's image.

6. Are there passages indicating that works are a witness?

There are three main passages:

- The first is aimed at people in the world who are observing disciples' conduct. They will be impressed by their care and concern for each other (John 13:35).

- The other two concern the general impact disciples have on the world around them (Matthew 5:16; 1 Peter 2:11-15). Good works here are a witness, a light in a dark world. Note that *"works"* are not just helping the poor and needy but encompass the entire life and character of the believer. This is consistent with James where his examples of faith expressed in works are not simply those of helping the poor, but include Abraham's offering of Isaac and Rahab's hiding the spies (James 2:14-26).

7. One method of preaching is to use good works as a means of meeting people. Through a programme of witnessing through charitable deeds a relationship with individuals is built up and then we start preaching the gospel. Is this approach scriptural?

At first sight it is an attractive idea. But it has to be said there are a number of differences from the scriptural principles we have identified:

- We cannot find any scriptural support for putting good works first and preaching second. New Testament teaching and example is the other way round: the mission of disciples is to preach the gospel and as they encounter needs they do what they can to help.
- Good works are an act of love, generated by seeing a problem we can help solve. Using good works as a preaching tool is not part of scriptural teaching.
- The Lord Jesus teaches us to *"Take heed that you do not do your charitable deeds before men"* (Matthew 6:1).
- Can it be possible to build a relationship with someone first and *then* start talking about what we believe? Surely our beliefs are what we are, they are our life, the basis of all our relationships.

There is no doubt about the sincerity and enthusiasm that lies behind this preaching method and both of these are essential. The next stage for each of us is to be confident in our own minds that our enthusiasm is expressed in accordance with the Master's teaching. Everything we do is a witness and our method of preaching is no exception. It must capture the urgency of our message and the need for men and women to be saved. The Bible must be at the forefront of our dealings with other people. The overwhelming priority is to bring life to a dying world and that must show itself in both how and what we preach.

Conclusion

Love expressed in action is the very pinnacle of our life in Christ. It is an unreserved, limitless love that is always ready to give and to serve. The believer's life will reflect the love that has been (and is still) shown to us by God through the Lord Jesus Christ. Jesus *"did not please himself"* but devoted his life to the service of others to meet their spiritual and material needs. As his disciples we try to follow his example.

Our priority is the eternal welfare of those around us. Inevitably in this present world we shall also encounter material needs of many kinds. Our immediate response will be to do what we can to alleviate the difficulty while remembering that the problems of this present age will not be removed until the kingdom of God is established.

Outline answers to questions

James chapter 1
1. I wish you joy.
2. To help us grow to spiritual maturity.
3. The human heart.
4. Being set free by grace leads to keeping God's commandments.
5. Be doers of the word!

James chapter 2:1-13
1. A synagogue.
2. God's possession of His people.
3. Because it will be the fundamental law of the kingdom of God.
4. *Agapē*.
5. Show mercy to others.

James chapter 2:14-26
1. Faith without works.
2. The *Shema*.
3. People who were mentally ill.
4. God asked him to offer Isaac.
5. Jericho.

James chapter 3
1. Its impact is out of proportion to its size.
2. The cycle of life, the day to day round of human activity.
3. The four groups of creatures were put under man's control at creation.
4. The human heart.
5. Peaceable.

James chapter 4
1. The fight against each disciple's natural instincts.
2. We should pray that God is glorified.
3. He left the world behind and developed a living faith.
4. Our plans are *"if the Lord will"*.
5. We must do it!

James chapter 5
1. The Romans destroying Jerusalem in AD 70 and the subsequent persecution of Jews.
2. The prophets and Job.
3. Come to God in prayer.
4. It should be fervent.
5. You save a soul from death and cover a multitude of sins.

Further reading

Further reading
If this Study Guide has got you thinking about the letter of James, and has increased your appetite for further study, you may wish to consider the following material.
- Neville Smart, *The Epistle of James* (Birmingham, *The Christadelphian*, 1955). With a layout similar to this Study Guide, this commentary, after three introductory chapters, examines all the individual sections of the letter. It contains its own select bibliography.
- Douglas J. Moo, *Tyndale New Testament Commentary: The Letter of James* (Inter-Varsity Press, Leicester, 1985). This detailed commentary provides plenty of factual information, although there are doctrinal differences between Christadelphians and Professor Moo.

NOTES

NOTES